WARRIOR MOM

"Defending Your Children in the Court of Heaven"

TIMOTHY ATUNNISE

GLOVIM PUBLISHING HOUSE
ATLANTA, GEORGIA

WARRIOR MOM

Copyright © 2023 by Timothy Atunnise

All rights reserved. No part of this book may be reproduced, copied, stored or transmitted in any form or by any means – graphic, electronic, or mechanical, including photocopying, recording, or information storage and retrieval systems without the prior written permission of Glovim Publishing House except where permitted by law.

Glovim Publishing House
1078 Citizens Pkwy
Suite A
Morrow, Georgia 30260

glovimbooks@gmail.com
www.glovimonline.org

Printed in the United States of America

Appreciation

Thank you for purchasing and reading my book. I am extremely grateful and hope you found value in reading it. Please consider sharing it with friends and family and leaving a review online.

Your feedback and support are always appreciated and allow me to continue doing what I love.

Please go to htttps://www.amazon.com/dp/B0CFX87CB2 if you'd like to leave a review.

Table of Contents

Introduction 7
The making of a warrior mom 10
The calling of a warrior mom 13
Understanding the battlefield 21
The court of heaven 29
Recognizing the enemy 36
Battle strategies 43
Step-by-step journey into the court of heaven 68
Your child's defender 81
The power of a mother's prayer 87
Unleashing divine power for your children's protection 94
A mother's guide to fighting for her children 109
The mother's mandate 137
Battle against the spirit of the street 153
War against the spirit of sexual perversion 171
The armor of God and how to use it 188
Utilizing spiritual authority 194
Shattering strongholds 200
Speaking life over your children 206
Safeguarding your child's destiny 212
From schoolyards to sleepovers 218
Releasing your child from wounds 224
Hope and strategies for wayward children 230
Guiding your children through life challenges 236
The joy of victory 242
Nurturing godly character in your children 246
Praise as warfare 251
Stories of warrior moms in action 255
Raising the next generation of warriors 259
The power of unity 263

Warrior moms in the Bible 267
Dealing with disappointments and setbacks 271
Trusting God in the midst of battle 277
victorious legacy 282
Your child, your heritage 286
Recognizing the signs of spiritual warfare 290
Praying with purpose and power 295
Defending your family from attacks 299
The art of spiritual self-care...302
Understanding the spiritual calendar 306
Other bestselling books from the author............................312

Introduction

In the realms where love and protection intertwine, a legion of extraordinary mothers rises, emboldened by an unyielding devotion to their children. These remarkable women understand that battles are not only fought on earthly terrain but also in the ethereal realm of the divine. They are Warrior Moms, fierce and unrelenting, engaging in spiritual warfare on their knees through the power of prayer.

In this groundbreaking spiritual warfare book, "Warrior Moms – Defending Your Children in the Court of Heaven," we delve into a world where mothers become spiritual warriors, challenging the forces that threaten the well-being and destiny of their precious ones. Drawing strength from the heavenly courts, these mothers enter into a dimension where prayer becomes a weapon, and intercession a potent force for change.

In this age of uncertainty and turmoil, the role of a mother is more crucial than ever. However, the battlefield has expanded beyond what meets the eye. It is a spiritual battleground where unseen forces seek to wreak havoc upon innocent lives. Warrior Moms recognize the urgency of the situation and are determined to defend their children against the onslaught of darkness.

Within the pages of this prayer book, you will discover an arsenal of prayers meticulously crafted to empower mothers in their divine calling. Whether your child faces physical ailments, emotional challenges, or spiritual warfare, these prayers will equip you to navigate the intricacies of the battlefield with unwavering resolve. From protection and guidance to healing and deliverance, the prayers within are specifically designed to target the unique needs of your child.

Each prayer is infused with an anointing of authority, as Warrior Moms rise up with boldness, addressing the heavenly court. They stand as intercessors, appealing to the Judge of all judges, presenting their petitions and requests on behalf of their children. These mothers recognize that the court of heaven holds the power to render verdicts that transcend earthly limitations.

Moreover, this prayer book embraces the pulse of the modern era. Weaving together timeless wisdom with contemporary insights, it illuminates the path to victory in a language that resonates with today's Warrior Moms. From viral hashtags to trending concepts, we bridge the gap between the spiritual and digital worlds, fostering a community of mothers united in their divine mission.

With stunning imagery and heart-stirring anecdotes, "Warrior Moms – Defending Your Children in the Court of Heaven" captures the essence of motherhood's warrior spirit. It celebrates the resilience, love, and audacity found within the hearts of mothers who refuse to be passive spectators in the battle for their children's destinies.

This book is not just a compilation of prayers; it is a call to action. It imparts the knowledge, confidence, and strategies needed to embark on a journey of spiritual warfare, transforming ordinary moms into formidable forces of intercession. In the midst of darkness, Warrior Moms rise as beacons of light, championing their children's futures with fervent prayer and unwavering faith.

So, dear Warrior Mom, join us on this extraordinary adventure. Let us embrace the power of warfare prayer and storm the gates of heaven together. As we forge ahead, fearlessly defending our children, we become an unstoppable force, igniting hope, and ushering in divine breakthroughs.

Welcome to "Warrior Moms – Defending Your Children in the Court of Heaven," where mothers become warriors, prayers become weapons, and victories become reality.

Foreword:

The Making of a Warrior Mom

Imagine being an empowered defender, standing as a protective barrier between your precious children and the challenges of a spiritual world unseen by human eyes. Picture yourself armed with faith and resilience, wearing the armor of God and unyielding in the face of adversities. This is the portrait of a "Warrior Mom", and it is a role that you, as a mother, are called to embrace.

"Warrior Mom: Defending Your Children in the Court of Heaven" is a call to arms, an invitation to engage in the spiritual battle for your children's destinies, health, happiness, and spiritual well-being. This is a book about warfare, not of swords and shields, but of faith, prayer, and love. It is about understanding that the struggle is not against flesh and blood, but against the rulers, authorities, and spiritual forces of evil in heavenly realms (Ephesians 6:12).

The Court of Heaven, as used in the title, is a term used to describe the spiritual realm where God, as the righteous Judge, renders decisions on behalf of His children. This term brings to mind the importance of prayer, as it is through prayer that we present our cases, our pleas for our children, before the Judge of all the earth.

In this book, you will learn how to engage in spiritual warfare strategically and effectively. You will learn to wield the Word of God like a sword, to use faith as a shield, and prayer as both offense and defense. You will learn how to discern the enemy's tactics, recognize spiritual attacks, and combat them with divine weapons.

Chapter by chapter, this book will guide you on how to defend your children in the Court of Heaven. It will introduce you to the concept of the Court of Heaven, explore the nature of spiritual warfare, and walk you through the process of standing in the gap for your children.

The first few chapters delve into the foundations of spiritual warfare, providing a solid understanding of what it entails. You will learn about the spiritual realm, discernment, and the importance of recognizing your authority in Christ.

The heart of the book lies in teaching you how to pray with power and purpose. You will uncover the principles of intercessory prayer, learn about the art of petitioning, and understand how to utilize your spiritual authority. You will learn how to use declarations, speak life over your children, and guard their destinies.

The following chapters will guide you in the daily application of these principles. You'll explore how to incorporate spiritual warfare in the everyday experiences of your children, from their school lives to their friendships. You will discover how to guide them through life's challenges using divine wisdom and how to nurture godly character in them.

This book is not just about battles; it also celebrates victories. You'll read about testimonies of triumph and stories of Warrior Moms who stood their ground and emerged victorious. As you read these stories, they will inspire you and assure you that victory is possible, and it is your portion in Christ.

Finally, the book will prepare you for the future. It will help you to raise the next generation of spiritual warriors and prepare you to pass on the baton when the time comes. It will teach you how to trust God amidst battles, deal with setbacks, and leave a victorious legacy for your children.

This journey will require courage, determination, and steadfast faith. It will not always be easy, but the victory will be glorious. For the battle belongs to the Lord, and He fights for His children. You are not alone in this fight. You are backed by the host of heaven, equipped by God, and empowered by His Spirit.

In essence, "Warrior Mom: Defending Your Children in the Court of Heaven" is your handbook for spiritual warfare, your guide to intercession, and your companion on this divine journey of motherhood. It is time to rise, Warrior Mom. Your children need you, and heaven is cheering you on.

Chapter 1

The Calling of a Warrior Mom

Every great journey begins with a calling. The calling of a Warrior Mom is no ordinary summons; it is a divine invitation, a holy mandate that arises from the depths of a mother's love, transcending the physical to touch the spiritual. The Warrior Mom's calling echoes through the corridors of heaven and reverberates in the chambers of her heart, reminding her of her sacred role as the protector, nurturer, and defender of her children.

This calling is not one of ordinary circumstances. It transcends the mundane, the everyday, the commonplace. It's not merely about packing healthy lunches, overseeing homework, or ensuring your children are safe on the playground. While these tasks are essential, the calling of a Warrior Mom beckons her into a grander arena, a spiritual battlefield where victories and losses have eternal consequences.

Let's begin our exploration of this calling by understanding its essence. The word "warrior" denotes someone engaged in or experienced in warfare; a person who shows or has shown great vigor, courage, or aggressiveness. The word "mom" conjures images of nurturing, caring, and gentle guidance. Combine these words, and you have a powerful portrait of a woman who fights valiantly for the welfare of her children, a force to be reckoned with. This is your calling.

The calling of a Warrior Mom is rooted in love. Love is the driving force behind her willingness to stand in the gap, to intercede, to wage war in the spiritual realm for her children's sake. This love isn't a fleeting feeling or a momentary affection. It is a profound, self-sacrificing love that mirrors God's love for His children.

This love is what pushes a Warrior Mom into the battlefield, ready to wage war against any forces that threaten her children's spiritual well-being. Just as a lioness defends her cubs with ferocious intensity, a Warrior Mom stands guard over her children, ready to face any enemy head-on. She becomes an immovable pillar of strength and faith, a beacon of light in a sometimes dark world.

But how does this calling come? It isn't marked by a grand spectacle or a blazing sign in the sky. Instead, it often arrives in the quiet, unnoticed moments. It could be in the early morning hours when you're praying for your child as they sleep, or in the quiet night when you're interceding for a wayward teenager. It could be the moment you realize that your battle for your children extends beyond the physical and into the spiritual realm.

Perhaps you've noticed that there are obstacles and challenges that your children face that you can't explain away as mere coincidence or bad luck. You've seen a pattern of struggles, a cycle of failures, or a string of disappointments that go beyond the ordinary. Or maybe you've discerned a spiritual attack against your family, or you've perceived a generational curse that seems to affect your children.

This awareness of the spiritual battleground is often the first step toward the calling of a Warrior Mom. It's the point where you become conscious of the need to arm yourself spiritually to defend your children in a realm unseen by the physical eye.

Answering this call means embracing a new dimension of motherhood, one where you accept the responsibility to spiritually cover your children in prayer and arm them with the knowledge of God's Word. It means becoming a prayer warrior, someone who is unafraid to engage in spiritual warfare and is equipped to stand in the gap for her children.

Being a Warrior Mom means recognizing that your children are not just flesh and blood, but they are spiritual beings with a divine destiny. You understand that as their mother, you have a unique role to play in guiding them towards this destiny. You understand that you're not just fighting for their present, but for their future, and for generations to come.

You start to realize the power of your prayers, the weight of your words, and the authority you have in Christ. You understand that your prayers can move mountains, tear down strongholds, and set up divine protections around your children.

You become more attuned to the spiritual climate around your children. You start to discern the enemy's tactics, and you can identify spiritual attacks. You learn to counter these attacks with the Word of God, to speak life over your children, and to pray protection over them.

While this calling is sacred, it is by no means an easy path to tread. The enemy is cunning and relentless. He seeks to steal, kill, and destroy (John 10:10). As a Warrior Mom, you're often on the frontline, shielding your children from these attacks. But take heart! You're not standing in your own strength; you're standing in the power of God, in the authority given to you through Christ Jesus.

Ultimately, the calling of a Warrior Mom is an ongoing journey. It's not a one-time event or a brief season. It's a lifelong commitment, a pledge to continually wage war in the spiritual realm on behalf of your children. This journey is paved with prayer, marked by faith, and fueled by love.

As you answer the call, you will find that you're not alone. You are backed by the host of heaven, equipped by God, and empowered by His Spirit. You are not just a mother; you are a Warrior Mom, and your battle cry is heard in heaven.

In this calling, you will discover a strength you never knew you had, a faith that stands unwavering in the face of trials, and a love that is fierce and unyielding. So, embrace your calling. Stand tall, Warrior Mom. The battle is the Lord's, but the fight... the fight is ours. And it is a fight we engage in with unwavering resolve, for the sake of our children, our legacy, and our faith.

"Pray in the language of heaven (Pray in tongues) for at least 10 minutes as you enter into the court of heaven to plead you case; if you cannot pray in tongues, enter His court with praise and worship for at least 10 minutes before you plead your case."

Warfare Prayers:

1. Heavenly Father, I declare that I am a warrior mom, called and anointed by you to fight in the spiritual realm for the well-being and protection of my children.
2. In the name of Jesus, I take authority over every force of darkness that seeks to harm or hinder my children's lives. I bind and rebuke every demonic influence and render them powerless.
3. I declare that my children are covered by the blood of Jesus, and no weapon formed against them shall prosper. I release the power of the cross into their lives, bringing them freedom, healing, and deliverance.
4. Lord, I pray that you surround my children with your mighty angels, forming a hedge of protection around them. I command every evil spirit to flee from their presence, for they dwell in the secret place of the Most High.

5. I declare that my children walk in divine health and wholeness. I speak against any sickness, disease, or infirmity that tries to come upon them. By the stripes of Jesus, they are healed.
6. Heavenly Father, I declare that my children have sound minds and are filled with the wisdom of God. I pray against any form of mental or emotional torment, and I release peace, joy, and stability into their hearts and minds.
7. I declare that my children are shielded from the influences of the world. I pray that they have discerning hearts and make wise choices, rejecting anything that goes against your Word.
8. Lord, I bind and break every generational curse and negative pattern that may be affecting my children's lives. I release the power of your redemption and restoration, setting them free from every bondage.
9. I declare that my children are overcomers. They are more than conquerors through Christ who strengthens them. I speak victory over every challenge they face, knowing that you are their ever-present help.
10. Heavenly Father, I pray for divine connections and godly friendships for my children. I declare that they are surrounded by people who will encourage, inspire, and support them in their journey of faith.
11. I take authority over any addiction or harmful habits that may try to entangle my children. I declare freedom and deliverance from every bondage, for whom the Son sets free is free indeed.

12. Lord, I pray that my children have a heart for you and a passion to seek your face. I declare that they have a deep hunger for your Word and a desire to walk in obedience to Your commands.
13. I declare that my children are anointed for their purpose. I speak blessings over their gifts, talents, and abilities, and I pray that they will use them to bring glory to your name.
14. Heavenly Father, I pray for divine protection over my children's minds. I bind and cast out every spirit of fear, doubt, and insecurity. I release the spirit of love, power, and a sound mind upon them.
15. I declare that my children are victorious in their spiritual battles. I pray that they put on the full armor of God and stand firm against the schemes of the enemy. They are more than conquerors in Christ.
16. Lord, I declare that my children have a heart of worship. I pray that they will experience your presence in a powerful way and that their worship will bring breakthrough and transformation in their lives.
17. I declare that my children have a spirit of excellence. They excel in their academics, relationships, and every area of their lives. I pray that they become leaders and influencers in their generation.
18. Heavenly Father, I pray for divine guidance and direction for my children. I declare that they hear your voice clearly and follow your path for their lives. You are their Shepherd, and they shall not lack any good thing.

19. I declare that my children have a heart of compassion and love for others. I pray that they become agents of change in their communities, spreading your love and kindness wherever they go.
20. Lord, I pray for supernatural favor upon my children. I declare open doors, divine opportunities, and blessings that surpass all understanding. Your favor goes before them and makes a way where there seems to be no way.
21. I take authority over every negative influence or peer pressure that may come against my children. I declare that they have the courage to stand firm in their convictions and make godly choices.
22. Heavenly Father, I pray for divine protection over my children's relationships. I declare that they are surrounded by godly friends and mentors who will speak life and truth into their lives.
23. I declare that my children walk in purity and integrity. I pray against any form of immorality or impurity and release the power of holiness and righteousness in their lives.
24. Lord, I pray for supernatural provision for my children's needs. I declare that you are their provider, and they shall lack nothing. Your abundance flows into their lives, meeting every need according to your riches in glory.
25. I declare that my children fulfill their destinies and purposes in Christ. I release blessings and favor over their lives, and I declare that they will impact the world for your kingdom. In Jesus' mighty name, Amen.

Chapter 2

Understanding the Battlefield: The Spiritual Realm

The role of a warrior is irrevocably intertwined with the battlefield upon which they fight. For a Warrior Mom, that battlefield is not of this physical world, but rather it exists in the spiritual realm, a reality running parallel to our own yet invisible to the naked eye. This chapter uncovers the realities of the spiritual realm, the battlefield that is the arena for spiritual warfare.

The spiritual realm may be unseen, but its impact upon our lives is very tangible. To understand the spiritual realm is to step into a reality that transcends our physical senses, one that extends beyond what we can touch, see, or hear. It is an eternal dimension where spiritual entities dwell, both the heavenly host and the forces of darkness. It is where prayers are heard, where angels move at God's command, and where battles for human souls are fought.

The Bible is rich with references to this spiritual realm. In the Old Testament, the prophet Elisha prayed that his servant's eyes might be opened to see this spiritual reality. In response, God allowed the servant to see a host of heavenly warriors ready for battle (2 Kings 6:17). This instance showcases that the spiritual realm coexists with our physical reality, and these two dimensions often interact.

Understanding the spiritual realm requires acknowledging its inhabitants. This realm is teeming with spiritual beings, both benevolent and malevolent. On the side of heaven, there are God, Jesus, the Holy Spirit, angels, and the great cloud of witnesses spoken of in Hebrews 12:1. Against them, there are Satan and his demonic forces, fallen angels who chose to rebel against God.

Satan, or the devil, is described in the Bible as a roaring lion seeking whom he may devour (1 Peter 5:8). He is the instigator of deceit, the father of lies (John 8:44), and the one who comes to steal, kill, and destroy (John 10:10). His demonic forces assist him in his evil mission, influencing individuals, societies, and even generations, seeking to divert them from the truth of God and His love.

The spiritual realm is also the domain where spiritual warfare occurs. Spiritual warfare is the conflict that happens in this spiritual realm, the struggle between the forces of God and the forces of Satan. Ephesians 6:12 states, "For our struggle is not against flesh and blood, but against the rulers, against the authorities, against the powers of this dark world and against the spiritual forces of evil in the heavenly realms." This verse illuminates the true nature of our battles as believers and particularly as Warrior Moms.

Recognizing the spiritual realm and understanding spiritual warfare is not about becoming fearful or overly focused on the enemy and his tactics. Instead, it's about gaining a clearer perspective of the bigger picture. It's about understanding that our physical world is influenced by this spiritual realm and that our prayers as Warrior Moms have significant spiritual impact.

This realization is both empowering and humbling. It's empowering because you become aware of the powerful role you play in this spiritual battle for your children. It's humbling because it reminds you that this battle is not in your strength but in God's.

Understanding the spiritual realm also brings clarity to the power of prayer. Prayer is not just a religious routine or a hopeful wish; it is a spiritual weapon. In prayer, you engage with God in the spiritual realm, you wage war against the enemy's plots, and you assert the victory of Christ over your children's lives.

As you pray, you create a spiritual canopy of protection over your children, one that shields them from the enemy's attacks. You release God's power to work in their lives, you enforce God's promises over them, and you thwart the enemy's plans for them.

In the spiritual realm, your words carry weight. When you declare God's Word over your children, you release spiritual power. The book of Proverbs 18:21 tells us, "Death and life are in the power of the tongue."

Your declarations of faith, of hope, and of victory can shape your children's destiny. They have the power to dismantle the enemy's plans and to establish God's will.

In the spiritual realm, faith is your currency. Hebrews 11:1 defines faith as the assurance of things hoped for, the conviction of things not seen. As a Warrior Mom, your faith isn't based on what you see in the physical realm but on the truth of God's Word and His promises. You learn to trust God in the unseen, to believe His promises, and to stand in faith even when the circumstances look contrary.

So, as a Warrior Mom, how do you navigate this spiritual realm? You do it through a consistent prayer life, through regular Bible study, through cultivating a relationship with the Holy Spirit, and through a community of faith. You discern the spiritual climate around your children, you pray with authority, you declare God's Word, and you stand in faith.

The spiritual realm is indeed a vast and complex reality, but as a believer, you have a guide, the Holy Spirit. Jesus promised in John 16:13, "When the Spirit of truth comes, He will guide you into all truth." As you lean on the Holy Spirit, He will guide you in understanding the spiritual realm and engaging effectively in spiritual warfare.

In this spiritual realm, you're not a bystander; you're a participant. As a Warrior Mom, you're on the front lines, defending your children in the battlefield of prayer. Your prayers, your faith, and your spiritual authority have a profound impact in this realm. You are a spiritual force to be reckoned with, a Warrior Mom standing her ground in the spiritual realm, defending her children in the court of heaven.

"Pray in the language of heaven (Pray in tongues) for at least 10 minutes as you enter into the court of heaven to plead you case; if you cannot pray in tongues, enter His court with praise and worship for at least 10 minutes before you plead your case."

Warfare Prayers:

1. Heavenly Father, I declare that I am a warrior mom, equipped with the armor of God to stand against the spiritual forces of evil in the heavenly realms.
2. In the name of Jesus, I take authority over every demonic influence that seeks to harm my family. I declare that no weapon formed against us shall prosper.
3. I plead the blood of Jesus over my family, covering us from the top of our heads to the soles of our feet. Let the blood of Jesus cleanse and protect us from all evil.
4. I declare that my children are a heritage from the Lord, and I claim God's promises of protection, provision, and guidance over their lives.

5. I bind and rebuke every spirit of fear, doubt, and confusion that tries to attack my family. I release the peace of God that surpasses all understanding upon us.
6. I command every stronghold of addiction, bondage, and unhealthy patterns to be broken in the name of Jesus. My family is set free by the power of the Holy Spirit.
7. I declare that my home is a sanctuary of God's presence. I invite the Holy Spirit to dwell within these walls and fill every corner with His light and love.
8. I break and nullify every curse or negative word spoken against my family. I declare that we are blessed, and we walk in the favor of the Lord.
9. I release the power of forgiveness and reconciliation within my family. I declare that love and unity prevail in our relationships, and every division is mended.
10. I pray for divine wisdom and discernment to guide me as a mother. I declare that I am anointed to make godly decisions for my children and lead them in the ways of the Lord.
11. I declare that my children are protected from every physical and spiritual danger. No sickness, accident, or harm shall come near them.
12. I declare that my family is a light in this world, shining brightly with the love of Christ. I pray that through our lives, others may come to know and experience God's goodness.

13. I bind and cast out every spirit of rebellion and disobedience from my children's lives. I declare that they will honor and obey God's commandments and walk in righteousness.
14. I decree supernatural favor over my family's finances, careers, and businesses. I declare that we are blessed to be a blessing, and our resources will be used for God's kingdom purposes.
15. I declare that my prayers have power and authority in the spiritual realm. Every prayer I pray aligns with God's will and brings about breakthrough and transformation.
16. I declare that my family is covered by the shield of faith, and no fiery dart of the enemy can penetrate it. We walk in faith and victory in every circumstance.
17. I command every demonic assignment against my family's health to be broken. I release the healing power of Jesus Christ to flow through our bodies, restoring and renewing us.
18. I declare that my children are filled with the Holy Spirit and walk in the fruits of the Spirit. They manifest love, joy, peace, patience, kindness, goodness, faithfulness, gentleness, and self-control.
19. I bind and render powerless every spirit of depression, anxiety, and mental torment that tries to attack my family. We have the mind of Christ, and His peace guards our hearts and minds.
20. I declare that my family's steps are ordered by the Lord. We walk in divine guidance and divine appointments, and we fulfill the purposes God has for us.

21. I declare that my home is a place of worship and prayer. We open our hearts and invite the presence of God to move mightily in our midst.
22. I break and sever every ungodly soul tie and influence that hinders my family's spiritual growth. We are dedicated and set apart for God's purposes alone.
23. I declare that my family is a testimony of God's faithfulness and provision. We lack no good thing, and every need is met according to His glorious riches.
24. I declare that my family's relationships are marked by love, respect, and honor. We speak words of life and encouragement, building one another up in faith.
25. I declare that my family is victorious in every battle. We overcome by the blood of the Lamb and the word of our testimony. Our lives bring glory and honor to our Lord Jesus Christ.

Chapter 3

The Court of Heaven: A Spiritual Overview

The Court of Heaven, a concept that may seem abstract, even mystical to some, is a spiritual reality that offers a profound understanding of the way God operates in the spiritual realm. Just as the earthly courts operate on principles and procedures, so does the heavenly court. This chapter unveils the intricacies of the Court of Heaven, shedding light on the legalities of the spiritual realm and their implications on spiritual warfare.

To begin, let's comprehend the term itself. The "Court of Heaven" is not an arbitrary phrase; it is rooted in Biblical imagery. The prophet Daniel, in Daniel 7:10, gives an astounding depiction of this heavenly scene, saying, "A river of fire was flowing, coming out from before Him. Thousands upon thousands attended Him; ten thousand times ten thousand stood before Him. The court was seated, and the books were opened." Here, Daniel depicts a judicial setting in the spiritual realm, presided over by God Himself.

This depiction challenges our conventional understanding of prayer and spiritual warfare. It presents the idea that spiritual warfare is not just about hurling spiritual arrows at the enemy; it's also about presenting our cases before the Judge of all the Earth (Genesis 18:25). It is about coming before

God, laying out our petitions, presenting our evidence (which is the Word of God), and pleading our case.

As a Warrior Mom, understanding the Court of Heaven offers a new perspective on your spiritual role. You are not just a mother or a prayer warrior; you are also an advocate, pleading your children's cases before the Judge of Heaven.

So, how do you operate in the Court of Heaven? Firstly, you come with reverence. Hebrews 12:28-29 tells us, "Therefore, since we are receiving a kingdom that cannot be shaken, let us be thankful, and so worship God acceptably with reverence and awe, for our 'God is a consuming fire.'" This scripture sets the tone for our approach. We approach with reverence, recognizing the holiness of God, and with gratitude, acknowledging His goodness and mercy.

Secondly, you come in the name of Jesus. In the spiritual realm, names carry authority. Coming in the name of Jesus means coming in His authority. It's like being granted the Power of Attorney; you are legally authorized to act on behalf of Jesus, the Righteous One. Jesus assured us in John 14:13, "And I will do whatever you ask in my name, so that the Father may be glorified in the Son." When you pray in Jesus' name, you are operating under His legal and spiritual authority.

Thirdly, you come with the Word of God. Isaiah 55:11 assures us that God's Word will not return void, but it will accomplish what God desires and achieve the purpose for which He sent it. God's Word is your evidence in the Court of Heaven. As you pray God's promises over your children, you are presenting the Judge with His own words, His own promises.

Another aspect of the Court of Heaven is the role of the accuser. Revelation 12:10 identifies Satan as the accuser of the brethren who accuses them before God day and night. Satan seeks to bring charges against us, reminding God of our failures, our sins, and our shortcomings.

But take heart, Warrior Mom! We have an advocate in Jesus. 1 John 2:1 tells us, "If anybody does sin, we have an advocate with the Father—Jesus Christ, the Righteous One." Jesus stands in our defense, His blood testifying of our righteousness and redemption.

Operating in the Court of Heaven, then, is a matter of understanding our position in Christ. We come with boldness, yet with humility. We come in the authority of Jesus' name, yet recognizing it's not our righteousness but His. We present our petitions, plead our case using God's promises, and trust in the advocacy of Jesus.

As a Warrior Mom, when you start to see your prayers as legal transactions in the spiritual realm, you begin to pray with a new level of authority and expectancy. You understand that your prayers are not just spiritual wishes; they are legal decrees. You are not just asking; you are declaring, proclaiming, and enforcing God's will in the lives of your children.

This understanding of the Court of Heaven empowers you to fight more effectively for your children. It's not about shouting louder or praying longer; it's about praying strategically, praying according to God's Word, and praying in alignment with His will. It's about standing in the gap for your children, advocating for them in the spiritual realm, and enforcing God's plans and purposes for their lives.

Understanding the Court of Heaven is a game-changer in spiritual warfare. It offers a paradigm shift, moving from a warfare mentality to a courtroom mentality. It's about recognizing the legalities of the spiritual realm and leveraging them for victory. As a Warrior Mom, you are not helpless; you are an advocate. You're not just fighting; you are winning because your victory is assured in Christ.

The Court of Heaven is not a concept to be feared but understood and operated in. As you gain understanding, you become more effective in your prayers, more strategic in your spiritual warfare, and more confident in your spiritual authority. You are not just a participant in the spiritual realm; you are a force to be reckoned with, a Warrior Mom who knows her place and role in the Court of Heaven.

> ***"Pray in the language of heaven (Pray in tongues) for at least 10 minutes as you enter into the court of heaven to plead you case; if you cannot pray in tongues, enter His court with praise and worship for at least 10 minutes before you plead your case."***

Warfare Prayer:

1. In the name of Jesus, I declare that I am a warrior mom, empowered by the Holy Spirit to intercede on behalf of my family.
2. Heavenly Father, I come before your throne of grace, acknowledging your sovereignty and seeking your divine protection and guidance.
3. I declare that my home is a sanctuary, and I establish it as a place of spiritual warfare, where the enemy's plans are thwarted, and his influence is nullified.
4. By the power of the blood of Jesus, I break every generational curse and bondage that has been passed down through my family line.
5. I declare that my children are surrounded by a hedge of angelic protection, and no weapon formed against them shall prosper.
6. I bind every spirit of fear, doubt, and confusion that seeks to hinder my children's spiritual growth, and I release a spirit of faith, wisdom, and understanding upon them.
7. I renounce and reject any ungodly influence that may try to infiltrate my home, and I declare that only the light of Christ shines within its walls.
8. I plead the blood of Jesus over my family, covering us from the top of our heads to the soles of our feet, and I declare that no evil shall come near us.

9. I break every assignment of the enemy that seeks to steal, kill, and destroy the destiny and purpose of my children, and I release divine protection and provision over them.
10. I declare that my children are blessed and highly favored of the Lord, and I decree that they will walk in righteousness and fulfill their God-given calling.
11. I bind every spirit of rebellion and disobedience in the lives of my children, and I release a spirit of obedience and submission to God's Word.
12. I decree that my children will excel academically, socially, and spiritually, and they will be leaders and not followers in this world.
13. I break every chain of addiction, bondage, and oppression that may try to ensnare my children, and I release the power of deliverance and freedom upon them.
14. I declare that my children will be filled with the knowledge of God's love and grace, and they will have a personal relationship with Jesus Christ.
15. I bind every spirit of sickness, disease, and infirmity that may try to attack my children's bodies, and I release divine healing and restoration upon them.
16. I decree that my family will be united in love, harmony, and peace, and we will be a testimony of God's goodness and faithfulness.
17. I declare that my prayers are powerful and effective, and as I stand in the court of heaven, I petition for the salvation of my family members who have not yet received Jesus as their Lord and Savior.

18. I declare that my home is a place of worship, prayer, and spiritual growth, and the presence of God dwells richly within its walls.
19. I bind every spirit of division, strife, and discord that may try to infiltrate my family relationships, and I release a spirit of unity and reconciliation.
20. I decree that my family will be a lighthouse in our community, shining the light of Christ and drawing others into a relationship with Him.
21. I bind every spirit of poverty, lack, and financial struggle that may try to hinder the prosperity and provision of my family, and I release a spirit of abundance and blessings.
22. I declare that my family is set apart for God's purposes, and we will walk in holiness and righteousness all the days of our lives.
23. I break every word curse, negative declaration, and assignment of the enemy spoken against my family, and I release the power of God's Word to bring healing and restoration.
24. I decree that my prayers are like arrows, hitting their targets in the spiritual realm, dismantling the strongholds of the enemy, and releasing breakthrough and victory.
25. I thank you, Lord, for hearing and answering my prayers. I trust in your faithfulness and declare that my family is more than conquerors through Christ Jesus. In Jesus mighty name, amen.

Chapter 4

Recognizing the Enemy:
Discernment in Spiritual Warfare

A crucial aspect of any battle is recognizing your enemy. In the context of spiritual warfare, the enemy is not a person, a situation, or a set of circumstances; the enemy is Satan and his demonic forces. Recognizing the enemy is about understanding the nature, tactics, and strategies of these forces of darkness. This chapter aims to equip you, the Warrior Mom, with the discernment necessary to recognize and effectively combat the enemy in spiritual warfare.

Satan, the main antagonist in spiritual warfare, is no match for God. He is a created being, limited in power, knowledge, and presence. He was once an angel, named Lucifer, but pride led him to rebel against God, and he was cast down from heaven (Isaiah 14:12-15; Ezekiel 28:12-17). Satan's desire is to oppose God, to deceive, and to cause destruction. However, despite his malevolent intentions, he can only operate within the boundaries God allows.

The Bible gives us several descriptions of Satan. In John 8:44, he is referred to as a murderer and the father of lies, indicating his deadly intentions and deceptive nature. In 1 Peter 5:8, he is described as a roaring lion looking for someone to devour, highlighting his predatory instincts. In 2 Corinthians 11:14, Satan is said to masquerade as an angel of light, revealing his ability to counterfeit and deceive. Recognizing these characteristics of Satan is paramount in discerning his workings in our lives and the lives of our children.

Recognizing the enemy is also about identifying the enemy's tactics. One of Satan's primary tactics is deception. From the Garden of Eden, where he deceived Eve (Genesis 3:1-13), to the temptation of Jesus in the wilderness (Matthew 4:1-11), Satan has used deception to lure people away from God's truth. He twists truth, creates doubt, and promotes lies.

Another tactic of Satan is temptation. Satan tempts us to sin, to act independently of God, to gratify our fleshly desires at the expense of God's will. He presents sin as appealing, as beneficial, even as justifiable.

Satan also uses accusation and condemnation to keep us in a cycle of guilt and shame. He reminds us of our past sins, our failures, and our weaknesses. He tries to make us feel unworthy, unloved, and unforgiven, contrary to the truth of God's unconditional love and forgiveness (Romans 8:1).

So how do you, as a Warrior Mom, discern the enemy's workings? First, by knowing the Word of God. The Bible is our primary tool for discerning truth from lies. As you immerse yourself in God's Word, you build a reservoir of truth that enables you to recognize when Satan is peddling lies.

Secondly, by cultivating a relationship with the Holy Spirit. The Holy Spirit is our Helper, our Teacher, our Guide (John 14:26). He illuminates our understanding, quickens our spirit, and leads us into all truth. Through the Holy Spirit, we can discern the spiritual climate around us, including the activities of the enemy.

Lastly, through a lifestyle of prayer. Prayer is not just about talking to God; it's also about listening to Him. In prayer, we create an environment for God to speak to us, to reveal things to us, to give us discernment.

Recognizing the enemy is not about becoming paranoid or seeing a demon behind every bush. It's about being spiritually alert, understanding that we are in a spiritual battle, and being able to discern when and how the enemy is at work. It's about being so familiar with the truth that when a lie comes along, you can quickly identify and reject it.

As a Warrior Mom, your role is not just to pray for your children but to discern the spiritual battles they may be facing. You are the watchman on the wall, alert to the enemy's tactics and ready to counteract them with prayer and the Word of God.

Recognizing the enemy is a critical aspect of spiritual warfare. It's not just about knowing who the enemy is, but also understanding how he operates.

As you grow in discernment, you become more effective in your spiritual warfare, not only defending your children in the spiritual realm but also teaching them how to recognize and resist the enemy.

Spiritual discernment is not a gift for a selected few; it's a necessity for every believer. As a Warrior Mom, you are called to a place of discernment, to recognize the enemy's tactics and to counter them with the truth of God's Word and the power of prayer. You're not just defending your children in the court of heaven; you're equipping them to stand their ground, to discern the enemy's lies, and to live in victory.

"Pray in the language of heaven (Pray in tongues) for at least 10 minutes as you enter into the court of heaven to plead you case; if you cannot pray in tongues, enter His court with praise and worship for at least 10 minutes before you plead your case."

Warfare Prayers:

1. Heavenly Father, I come before you as a warrior mom, recognizing the spiritual battles that my family faces. I declare that I am discerning and vigilant in recognizing the enemy's tactics.
2. I take authority over every scheme of the enemy aimed at my children and family. I declare that no weapon formed against us shall prosper, and every tongue that rises against us in judgment shall be condemned.

3. In the name of Jesus, I bind every spirit of fear, doubt, and confusion that seeks to torment my family. I release the peace of God that surpasses all understanding to guard our hearts and minds.
4. I declare that my children are covered by the blood of Jesus. I plead the blood of Jesus over their lives, protecting them from any harm or evil assignment of the enemy.
5. By the power of the Holy Spirit, I discern and expose every hidden work of darkness attempting to infiltrate my family. I command every demonic stronghold to be exposed and broken in the name of Jesus.
6. I declare that my family walks in divine health and protection. I rebuke every sickness, disease, and infirmity, and I release the healing power of Jesus over our bodies.
7. I renounce and break every generational curse and stronghold that has been passed down in my family line. I declare freedom and deliverance from every bondage in the name of Jesus.
8. I declare that my family is surrounded by a hedge of angelic protection. I release ministering angels to guard and defend us against every attack of the enemy.
9. I declare that my children have a heart and mind that is receptive to the truth of God's Word. I pray that their spiritual discernment increases, and they are guided by the wisdom of the Holy Spirit.
10. I bind and cast out every spirit of rebellion and disobedience from my family. I declare that my children walk in obedience to God's commands and are protected from the consequences of sin.

11. I declare that my home is a sanctuary of God's presence. I rebuke every unclean spirit and release the atmosphere of heaven to permeate every room in our house.
12. I declare that my prayers have power and authority in the spiritual realm. I stand firm in faith, knowing that when I pray according to God's will, He hears and answers me.
13. I break every curse spoken against my children's destiny and purpose. I declare that they will fulfill the plans and purposes God has for their lives, walking in their true identity as sons and daughters of the Most High.
14. I declare that my family is a united front against the enemy. We stand together in love, forgiveness, and unity, refusing to allow division or strife to gain a foothold.
15. I pray a hedge of protection around my children's minds, guarding them from the deceptive influences of the enemy. I declare that their thoughts are aligned with God's truth and are filled with purity and righteousness.
16. I declare that my family is set apart for God's purposes. We are a light in the darkness, and wherever we go, we bring the presence and power of God with us.
17. I rebuke every spirit of addiction and bondage that seeks to ensnare my family members. I declare their freedom and deliverance from every form of captivity in the name of Jesus.
18. I declare divine favor over my family's lives. I pray that doors of opportunity open, and God's blessings and provision flow abundantly in every area of our lives.

19. I break every curse of failure and defeat that has been spoken over my family. I declare that we are more than conquerors through Christ Jesus, and we walk in victory in every circumstance.
20. I declare that my children are surrounded by godly influences and mentors who speak life and truth into their lives. I pray that they are guided by wise counsel and are protected from harmful relationships.
21. I declare that my family is marked by the love of Christ. We walk in forgiveness, compassion, and grace towards one another and extend that love to those around us.
22. I bind and rebuke every spirit of anxiety and worry that attempts to rob my family's peace. I release the peace of God that surpasses all understanding, guarding our hearts and minds in Christ Jesus.
23. I declare that my family's faith grows stronger with each passing day. We are rooted and grounded in the Word of God, and our trust in Him is unwavering.
24. I rebuke every spirit of discouragement and despair that seeks to attack my family. I release the spirit of hope, joy, and laughter into our lives, knowing that the joy of the Lord is our strength.
25. I declare that my family is a testimony of God's faithfulness and goodness. We overcome by the blood of the Lamb and the word of our testimony, and we give glory to God for His mighty works in our lives. In Jesus' name.

Chapter 5

Battle Strategies:
Warrior Mom's Handbook for Spiritual Warfare

Warrior moms engage in spiritual warfare, recognizing that the battles they face extend beyond the physical realm. They understand the importance of equipping themselves with spiritual armor and employing strategic tactics to protect their families and navigate the challenges of life. These warrior moms draw inspiration from the Scriptures, which provide them with timeless wisdom and guidance. In Ephesians 6:11-12, the apostle Paul writes, "Put on the full armor of God, so that you can take your stand against the devil's schemes. For our struggle is not against flesh and blood, but against the rulers, against the authorities, against the powers of this dark world and against the spiritual forces of evil in the heavenly realms." This passage reminds warrior moms that their ultimate battle is against spiritual forces, emphasizing the need for a comprehensive spiritual defense.

One of the key strategies employed by warrior moms is the power of prayer. They understand the significance of communicating with God, seeking His guidance, and interceding for their families. James 5:16 affirms the effectiveness of prayer, stating, "The prayer of a righteous person is powerful and effective." Warrior moms engage in fervent prayer, covering their children and loved ones with God's protection and blessings. They remain steadfast in their faith, knowing that their prayers have the power to bring about transformation and victory in the midst of spiritual battles.

In addition to prayer, warrior moms also immerse themselves in God's Word, utilizing it as a sword to combat the lies and deceptions of the enemy. Hebrews 4:12 declares, "For the word of God is alive and active. Sharper than any double-edged sword, it penetrates even to dividing soul and spirit, joints and marrow; it judges the thoughts and attitudes of the heart." Warrior moms arm themselves with the truth of Scripture, studying and meditating on it daily. They employ specific verses that speak to their battles, such as Psalm 91:11, which says, "For he will command his angels concerning you to guard you in all your ways." By anchoring themselves in God's Word, warrior moms gain strength, wisdom, and discernment to overcome spiritual challenges and protect their families.

Warrior moms engage in spiritual warfare by putting on the full armor of God, employing the power of prayer, and immersing themselves in God's Word. These battle strategies enable them to navigate the spiritual challenges they encounter and protect their families from the schemes of the enemy. By relying on the wisdom and guidance found in Scripture, warrior moms find strength, courage, and hope, knowing that God is their ultimate source of victory. As they abide in prayer and stand firm in their faith, they exemplify the heart of a true warrior mom, ready to face any battle that comes their way.

Battle Strategies

Prayer and Intercession

Prayer is a powerful tool in spiritual warfare. A warrior mom can regularly intercede on behalf of her children, seeking God's protection, guidance, and blessings for them. Praying for their spiritual growth, well-being, and safety can create a strong foundation in the court of heaven.

Before engaging in any spiritual battle, it is crucial to seek God's guidance, wisdom, and protection. Ask the Holy Spirit to lead you and reveal any specific strategies or scripture references that may apply to your situation. Rely on the power of the Holy Spirit to intercede on your behalf (Romans 8:26-27).

Declaration of Seeking Divine Wisdom:

Heavenly Father, I declare that I receive divine wisdom to pray for my children. According to James 1:5, I believe that if I lack wisdom, I can ask of you, who gives generously to all without finding fault. Grant me the discernment and understanding to intercede effectively for my children's needs and protection.

Declaration of Strength and Courage:

Mighty God, I declare that I receive strength and courage to pray boldly for my children. As it is written in Philippians 4:13, I can do all things through Christ who strengthens me. I choose to stand strong in faith and persistently lift up my children before your throne, knowing that you empower me to overcome any challenge.

Declaration of God's Protection:
Heavenly Father, I declare that I receive the assurance of your divine protection over my children. I claim your promise from Psalm 91:11, that you command your angels to guard and protect my children in all their ways. I trust in your unfailing love and commit my children into your mighty hands.

Declaration of Praying According to God's Will:
Lord, I declare that I receive the discernment to pray according to your will for my children. As I meditate on your Word, I align my prayers with your purposes. In 1 John 5:14-15, it is written that if we ask anything according to your will, you hear us, and if we know that you hear us, we have the petitions we desire of you. I trust in your perfect plan for my children's lives.

Declaration of God's Promises for Your Children:
Heavenly Father, I declare that I receive the confidence to pray and claim your promises for my children. Your Word assures me in Isaiah 54:13 that all my children shall be taught by you, and great shall be their peace. I stand firm on your promises, believing that you are faithful to fulfill them. I declare your blessings and favor upon my children's lives.

Scripture and Declarations:

Utilize the power of Scripture by meditating on relevant verses and making declarations of God's promises over your children. Speak out affirmations of faith and claim God's protection, favor, and blessings for them. This can help establish a spiritual covering over your children and combat any negative influences.

Find scriptures that speak of God's promises for your children and declare them in your prayers. For example, Jeremiah 29:11 says, "For I know the plans I have for you, declares the Lord, plans to prosper you and not to harm you, plans to give you hope and a future." Proclaim these promises with faith, believing that God's Word is powerful and effective (Hebrews 4:12).

Declaration of Protection:
Heavenly Father, I declare your promise of protection over my children. I thank you that they dwell in the secret place of the Most High, and they abide under the shadow of the Almighty. No evil shall befall them, and no plague shall come near their dwelling, for you have commanded your angels to guard them in all their ways. (Psalm 91:1-2, 10-11)

Declaration of Guidance:
Lord, I declare your promise of guidance over my children. I thank you that you will instruct them and teach them in the way they should go; you will counsel them with your loving eye upon them. I trust that they will

hear your voice behind them, saying, 'This is the way; walk in it.' (Psalm 32:8, Isaiah 30:21)

Declaration of Strength:

Heavenly Father, I declare your promise of strength over my children. I thank you that you are their refuge and strength, an ever-present help in trouble. I believe that they can do all things through Christ who strengthens them. They will soar on wings like eagles; they will run and not grow weary; they will walk and not be faint. (Psalm 46:1, Philippians 4:13, Isaiah 40:31)

Declaration of Wisdom:

Lord, I declare your promise of wisdom over my children. I thank you that if they lack wisdom, they can ask you, and you will give it generously without finding fault. I believe that your wisdom will guide them in making right decisions, and they will walk in understanding and discernment. (James 1:5, Proverbs 3:13)

Declaration of Salvation:

Heavenly Father, I declare your promise of salvation over my children. I thank you that you desire for all to be saved and come to the knowledge of the truth. I trust that you are drawing my children to yourself and that they will confess with their mouths that Jesus is Lord and believe in their hearts that you raised him from the dead, and they will be saved. (1 Timothy 2:3-4, Romans 10:9)

Pray for Protection and Deliverance:

Pray specifically for your children's protection and deliverance from any spiritual principalities and powers that may be negatively influencing their lives. Use scriptures such as Psalm 91 to declare God's protection over them and ask for His intervention.

Declaration of God's Protection:

Heavenly Father, I declare your divine protection over my children, shielding them from all demonic influences. In the name of Jesus, I rebuke every evil spirit that seeks to harm or oppress them. I stand on the promise of Psalm 91:11: 'For he will command his angels concerning you to guard you in all your ways.'

Declaration of Freedom from Bondage:

Lord Jesus, I declare freedom for my children from every form of demonic bondage. By the power of your blood shed on the cross, I break every chain that holds them captive. I claim the truth of Galatians 5:1: 'It is for freedom that Christ has set us free. Stand firm, then, and do not let yourselves be burdened again by a yoke of slavery.'

Declaration of Spiritual Authority:

Mighty God, I declare my authority as a parent in Christ, to enforce your victory over the enemy in my children's lives. I take hold of the promise in Luke 10:19: 'I have given you authority to trample on snakes and scorpions and to overcome all the power of the enemy; nothing will harm you.' I command every demonic stronghold to be shattered in Jesus' name.

Declaration of Renewed Mind:

Gracious Father, I declare a renewed mind for my children, free from the lies and deceptions of the enemy. I claim the power of Romans 12:2: 'Do not conform to the pattern of this world but be transformed by the renewing of your mind. Then you will be able to test and approve what God's will is—his good, pleasing, and perfect will.'

Declaration of God's Love and Identity:

Heavenly Father, I declare that my children are loved and cherished by you. I renounce every spirit of fear, rejection, and insecurity that seeks to torment them. I declare the truth of 1 John 4:18: 'There is no fear in love. But perfect love drives out fear.' I affirm that my children are children of God, fearfully and wonderfully made.

Spiritual Discernment:

Develop discernment to recognize spiritual battles and attacks that may affect your children. Stay vigilant and sensitive to any signs of spiritual opposition or negative influences in their lives. Trust your intuition and seek guidance from the Holy Spirit to discern the strategies of the enemy.

Prayer Declaration 1:

Heavenly Father, I declare and decree that my children are protected from all spiritual battles and attacks. I ask for discernment to recognize any schemes of the enemy that may affect them. Your Word says in Psalm 91:11-12, 'For he will command his angels concerning you to guard you in all your ways. On their hands they will bear you up, lest you strike your foot against a stone.' I trust in Your divine protection over my children.

Prayer Declaration 2:
Lord, I declare that my children are filled with the Holy Spirit, who grants them wisdom and discernment. I pray that they are sensitive to the leading of the Holy Spirit and can recognize any spiritual battles or attacks that may come their way. Your Word assures us in James 1:5, 'If any of you lacks wisdom, let him ask God, who gives generously to all without reproach, and it will be given him.' I thank You for imparting discernment upon my children.

Prayer Declaration 3:
Heavenly Father, I declare that my children walk in the light of Your truth. I pray that their spiritual eyes are opened to discern between good and evil, and that they are not deceived by the enemy's tactics. Your Word says in John 8:32, 'And you will know the truth, and the truth will set you free.' I declare that my children are anchored in Your truth, and they discern and reject any falsehood.

Prayer Declaration 4:
Lord, I declare that my children are covered by the armor of God, equipped for spiritual warfare. I pray that they develop discernment to recognize the enemy's attacks and stand firm against them. As it is written in Ephesians 6:11, 'Put on the whole armor of God, that you may be able to stand against

the schemes of the devil.' I thank You for empowering my children to discern and resist any spiritual attacks they may encounter.

Prayer Declaration 5:
Heavenly Father, I declare that my children are surrounded by a hedge of protection, shielded from any spiritual battles and attacks. I pray for discernment that allows them to see beyond the natural realm and perceive the spiritual realm. Your Word assures us in Psalm 34:7, 'The angel of the Lord encamps around those who fear him and delivers them.' I trust in Your faithfulness to guard and guide my children, giving them discernment in all circumstances.

Spiritual Cleansing:

Engage in regular spiritual cleansing for yourself and your children. This can involve confessing sins, renouncing any ungodly influences, and praying for spiritual cleansing and protection. Additionally, you can consider engaging in practices such as anointing your home with oil or using spiritual tools like holy water or blessed objects.

Declaration of Renouncing Ungodly Influences:
Heavenly Father, I come before you in the name of Jesus Christ, renouncing any ungodly influences in my life and the lives of my children. I declare that we will no longer be bound by the powers of darkness but will walk in the light of your truth and righteousness. I renounce all forms of witchcraft, idolatry, immorality, and every evil influence that seeks to

hinder our spiritual growth. By the authority of your Word, I break every chain and stronghold that has held us captive, and I declare freedom in Christ. Amen!

Scripture Reference:
Galatians 5:1 – "For freedom Christ has set us free; stand firm therefore, and do not submit again to a yoke of slavery."

Declaration of Spiritual Cleansing:
Gracious Lord, I humbly come before you, acknowledging our need for spiritual cleansing. Wash us with your precious blood, purify our hearts, and make us white as snow. I pray that you would remove any unclean spirits and ungodly influences from our lives. Fill us with your Holy Spirit, empowering us to live a life pleasing to you. Create in us a clean heart, O God, and renew a right spirit within us. In Jesus' name, I receive your cleansing and declare that we are set apart for your purposes. Amen!

Scripture References:
Psalm 51:10 – "Create in me a clean heart, O God, and renew a right spirit within me."
1 John 1:9 – "If we confess our sins, he is faithful and just to forgive us our sins and to cleanse us from all unrighteousness."

Declaration of Protection:
Lord, I lift up a prayer for the protection of myself and my children. I declare that no weapon formed against us shall prosper. I take refuge under

the shadow of your wings, and I trust in your unfailing love and mighty power. Guard us from all evil, both seen and unseen, and surround us with your heavenly angels. May your divine protection be a shield around us, keeping us safe from harm. In Jesus' name, I declare victory over every scheme of the enemy. Amen!

Scripture References:
Isaiah 54:17 – "no weapon that is fashioned against you shall succeed, and you shall confute every tongue that rises against you in judgment."
Psalm 91:11 – "For he will command his angels concerning you to guard you in all your ways."

Declaration of Spiritual Discernment:
Heavenly Father, I pray for discernment for myself and my children. Grant us the ability to recognize and discern every ungodly influence that may come our way. Open our eyes to see through deceptive schemes and false teachings. Fill us with your wisdom and understanding, that we may make godly choices and walk in alignment with your Word. Holy Spirit, guide us into all truth and protect us from deception. In Jesus' name, I declare that we have the mind of Christ and discernment in all things. Amen!

Scripture References:
James 1:5 – "If any of you lacks wisdom, let him ask God, who gives generously to all without reproach, and it will be given him."
1 Corinthians 2:16 – "For who has understood the mind of the Lord so as to instruct him? But we have the mind of Christ."

Declaration of Victory and Authority:
Mighty God, I declare victory and authority over any ungodly influences that have tried to establish themselves in our lives. I affirm that Jesus Christ has given us power and authority over all the works of darkness. By the blood of Jesus, I break every generational curse and every chain that has bound us. I declare that we are more than conquerors through Christ who loves us. I walk in the authority you have given me and decree that we are free and victorious in every area of life. In Jesus' mighty name, I pray. Amen!

Scripture References:
Luke 10:19 – "Behold, I have given you authority to tread on serpents and scorpions, and over all the power of the enemy, and nothing shall hurt you."
Romans 8:37 – "No, in all these things we are more than conquerors through him who loved us."

Covering in the Blood of Jesus:

Plead the blood of Jesus over your children as a powerful spiritual weapon. Declare and believe in the protection and redemption that comes through the blood of Jesus. Visualize your children covered in the blood of Jesus, which serves as a spiritual shield against the enemy's attacks. Referencing scriptures such as Revelation 12:11 can reinforce this approach.

Heavenly Father, I declare and plead the blood of Jesus over my children, covering them with His divine protection and shielding them from any harm or evil influence. "And they overcame him by the blood of the Lamb and by the word of their testimony..." (Revelation 12:11)

Lord, I invoke the power of the blood of Jesus to cleanse my children from any sins, mistakes, or wrong choices they may have made. Let them walk in the freedom and forgiveness that comes through the blood of Christ. "But if we walk in the light as He is in the light, we have fellowship with one another, and the blood of Jesus Christ His Son cleanses us from all sin." (1 John 1:7)

Father, I claim the authority of the blood of Jesus over my children's minds, emotions, and thoughts. I declare that they have the mind of Christ and are protected from any negative influences that may try to distract or deceive them. "For 'who has known the mind of the Lord that he may instruct Him?' But we have the mind of Christ." (1 Corinthians 2:16)

In the name of Jesus, I plead the blood of Jesus over my children's physical bodies. I declare that they are healed, strong, and protected from any sickness, disease, or injury. "But He was wounded for our transgressions, He was bruised for our iniquities; the chastisement for our peace was upon Him, and by His stripes we are healed." (Isaiah 53:5)

Heavenly Father, I declare the power of the blood of Jesus over my children's future, their dreams, and their destinies. I pray that they will walk in the purpose and calling You have for their lives, and that no weapon formed against them shall prosper. "No weapon formed against you shall prosper, and every tongue which rises against you in judgment you shall condemn. This is the heritage of the servants of the Lord, and their righteousness is from Me, says the Lord." (Isaiah 54:17)

Engage Heavenly Authorities:

In the court of heaven, you can present your case before God, the ultimate judge. Declare your children's destinies and purpose, seeking heavenly mandates and assignments over their lives. Ask for angelic protection and intervention in their daily lives.

So, as a believer, you have been given authority in Christ (Luke 10:19). Pray with confidence, knowing that you have authority over spiritual forces. Command any principalities and powers that are negatively affecting your children to leave in the name of Jesus.

Heavenly Father, I declare that my children are protected by the power of Your angels, and no weapon formed against them shall prosper. I release Your divine authority over their lives. The Bible says, "For he will command his angels concerning you to guard you in all your ways." (Psalm 91:11)

In the name of Jesus, I declare that my children are destined for greatness and success. I declare that they are filled with wisdom and understanding, and they walk in the path of righteousness. The Bible says, "For I know the plans I have for you, declares the Lord, plans for welfare and not for evil, to give you a future and a hope." (Jeremiah 29:11)

I bind and rebuke any spirit of fear, doubt, and confusion that may try to hinder my children's destiny. I declare that they have a sound mind, strong faith, and unwavering confidence in God's purposes for their lives. The Bible says, "For God gave us a spirit not of fear but of power and love and self-control." (2 Timothy 1:7)

Heavenly Father, I declare that my children are surrounded by godly influences and divine connections. I declare that they walk in the light, separated from the darkness of this world, and that they are guided by Your Spirit in all their decisions. The Bible says, "Do not be deceived: 'Bad company ruins good morals.'" (1 Corinthians 15:33)

I declare that my children are overcomers in Christ Jesus. I declare that they are equipped with the armor of God, standing firm against the schemes of the enemy. I decree victory over every obstacle and challenge they may face. The Bible says, "No, in all these things we are more than conquerors through him who loved us." (Romans 8:37)

Put on the Armor of God:

In Ephesians 6:10-18, the Apostle Paul instructs believers to put on the full armor of God to stand against spiritual forces of evil. This armor includes the belt of truth, the breastplate of righteousness, the gospel of peace, the shield of faith, the helmet of salvation, and the sword of the Spirit, which is the Word of God. By equipping yourself with the armor of God, you can be prepared to intercede for your children.

Declaration of Truth:
I declare that I am equipped with the belt of truth, girding my loins with the Word of God. I am rooted in the truth, and the lies of the enemy have no power over me. Ephesians 6:14 says, 'Stand therefore, having fastened on the belt of truth.' I am strengthened by the truth of God's promises, and I reject the deceptive schemes of the devil.

Declaration of Righteousness:
I declare that I am covered with the breastplate of righteousness, protecting my heart and my motives. I have been made righteous through faith in Jesus Christ. Philippians 3:9 reminds me, 'And be found in him, not having a righteousness of my own that comes from the law, but that which comes through faith in Christ.' I walk in the righteousness of Christ, and I resist every accusation and condemnation of the enemy.

Declaration of Peace:
I declare that my feet are shod with the readiness of the gospel of peace. I am equipped to bring peace and reconciliation wherever I go. Romans 10:15 affirms, 'How beautiful are the feet of those who preach the good news!' I am an ambassador of peace, and I refuse to be swayed by the

discord and chaos of the enemy. I carry the message of hope and reconciliation to a hurting world.

Declaration of Faith:

I declare that I take up the shield of faith, extinguishing all the fiery darts of the evil one. Hebrews 11:1 reminds me, 'Now faith is the assurance of things hoped for, the conviction of things not seen.' I trust in the Lord with unwavering faith, and I reject doubt, fear, and discouragement. My faith is a shield that protects me from the enemy's attacks, and I stand firm in the promises of God.

Declaration of Salvation:

I declare that I wear the helmet of salvation, guarding my mind and my thoughts. I am saved by grace through faith in Jesus Christ. 1 Thessalonians 5:8 declares, 'But since we belong to the day, let us be sober, having put on the breastplate of faith and love, and for a helmet the hope of salvation.' I am secure in my salvation, and I reject every lie and temptation that seeks to undermine my identity in Christ.

Fellowship and Support:

Seek support from fellow believers who can join you in prayer and intercession for your children. Engage in fellowship with like-minded individuals who can provide guidance, encouragement, and accountability in your spiritual warfare journey. The Bible encourages us to pray together and bear one another's burdens (James 5:16, Galatians 6:2). The collective prayers of believers can have a powerful impact.

Heavenly Father, I declare that you will raise up a mighty army of prayer warriors to intercede for my children, covering them in prayer and spiritual protection. Your Word assures me in Isaiah 54:13 that all my children will be taught by you, and great will be their peace.

Lord, I proclaim that you will surround my children with godly influences and mentors who will guide them in the ways of righteousness. As it is written in Proverbs 13:20, "Walk with the wise and become wise, for a companion of fools suffers harm."

Almighty God, I declare that you will shield my children from the schemes of the enemy and deliver them from evil. Your Word assures me in Psalm 91:11-12 that you will command your angels to guard and protect them, ensuring that no harm comes near their dwelling.

Heavenly Father, I proclaim that you will grant my children discernment and wisdom to make godly choices in every area of their lives. Your Word declares in James 1:5 that if anyone lacks wisdom, they should ask of you, who gives generously to all without finding fault, and it will be given to them.

Lord, I declare that you will empower my children with spiritual strength and courage to stand firm in their faith. As Ephesians 6:10-11 reminds us,

"Finally, be strong in the Lord and in his mighty power. Put on the full armor of God so that you can take your stand against the devil's schemes."

"Pray in the language of heaven (Pray in tongues) for at least 10 minutes as you enter into the court of heaven to plead you case; if you cannot pray in tongues, enter His court with praise and worship for at least 10 minutes before you plead your case."

Warfare Prayers:

1. Heavenly Father, I come before you today in the name of Jesus to pray fervently for the protection of my children's destiny against the forces of darkness.
2. I declare that my children are surrounded by the hedge of divine protection, and no weapon formed against them shall prosper.
3. I bind and rebuke every spirit of fear, doubt, and confusion that may try to hinder my children's progress and destiny.
4. I release the power of God's love and peace over my children, so that they may walk in confidence and clarity of purpose.
5. I break and destroy every generational curse or negative pattern that may be operating in my children's lives, in Jesus' name.
6. I declare that my children are vessels of honor in the hands of God, and their destiny is secure in Him.
7. I take authority over every demonic assignment set against my children's destiny, and I render them null and void in Jesus' name.

8. I command every evil plan and plot of the enemy to be exposed and brought to naught concerning my children's destiny.
9. I release the fire of God to consume every evil altar or shrine erected against my children's future.
10. I decree divine alignment with the perfect will of God for my children's lives, and I break every yoke of bondage that may hinder their progress.
11. I bind and cast out every spirit of addiction, rebellion, or disobedience that may try to ensnare my children.
12. I plead the blood of Jesus over my children's minds, hearts, and bodies, protecting them from any form of harm or evil influence.
13. I pray for godly wisdom and discernment to be poured out upon my children, that they may make wise decisions and walk in the path of righteousness.
14. I decree that my children will excel in every area of their lives, academically, spiritually, emotionally, and socially.
15. I rebuke every spirit of failure or mediocrity that may try to hinder my children's progress, and I declare a spirit of excellence over their lives.
16. I break every curse of limitation or stagnation that may have been spoken over my children's lives, and I release them into a season of accelerated growth and advancement.
17. I bind and rebuke every spirit of sickness, disease, or infirmity that may try to attack my children's health, and I release divine healing over their bodies.

18. I pray for divine favor and open doors of opportunity for my children, that they may walk in the fullness of their destiny.
19. I declare that my children are filled with the Holy Spirit and empowered to overcome every obstacle or challenge they may face.
20. I take authority over every negative influence, peer pressure, or ungodly relationship that may try to steer my children away from their destiny, and I break its hold in Jesus' name.
21. I release the angels of God to surround and protect my children wherever they go, keeping them safe from all harm.
22. I pray for godly mentors and role models to be placed in my children's lives, guiding them in the right direction and helping them fulfill their purpose.
23. I rebuke every spirit of distraction or procrastination that may hinder my children from pursuing their dreams and goals.
24. I declare that my children will walk in integrity and righteousness, and they will be a light in the midst of darkness.
25. I pray for divine guidance and direction in every decision my children make, that they may align themselves with God's perfect plan for their lives.
26. I break every soul tie or unhealthy attachment that may bind my children to any person or situation that is not in alignment with their destiny.
27. I release the power of forgiveness and reconciliation in my children's relationships, that they may walk in unity and love.

28. I declare that my children are overcomers by the blood of the Lamb and the word of their testimony.
29. I pray for divine provision and abundance in every area of my children's lives, that they may have more than enough to fulfill their purpose.
30. I bind and rebuke every spirit of discouragement or hopelessness that may try to weigh down my children's spirits, and I release the joy of the Lord over their lives.
31. I decree divine protection over my children's dreams and visions, that they may be fulfilled according to God's perfect timing.
32. I pray for divine connections and divine appointments for my children, that they may meet the right people who will help propel them towards their destiny.
33. I release the power of God's Word over my children's lives, that it may be a lamp unto their feet and a light unto their path.
34. I declare that my children will walk in humility and teachability, always willing to learn and grow in wisdom.
35. I rebuke every spirit of laziness or complacency that may try to hinder my children's diligence and perseverance.
36. I pray for divine protection over my children's emotions and mental well-being, that they may be anchored in God's peace and joy.
37. I release the power of God's grace and mercy over my children, covering them in times of weakness or failure.

38. I decree divine breakthroughs and divine opportunities for my children, that they may soar to new heights and accomplish great things for God's glory.
39. I pray for divine restoration and restitution for anything that has been stolen or lost in my children's lives, that they may be fully restored to their rightful place.
40. I bind and rebuke every spirit of delay or hindrance that may try to obstruct my children's progress, and I release divine acceleration over their lives.
41. I decree that my children will be leaders and influencers in their generation, shining the light of Christ wherever they go.
42. I rebuke every spirit of pride or self-centeredness that may try to hinder my children's humility and servant-heartedness.
43. I pray for divine protection over my children's dreams and aspirations, that they may be shielded from the attacks of the enemy.
44. I release the power of God's anointing over my children's lives, that they may walk in supernatural favor and authority.
45. I decree divine restoration and healing in any area of my children's lives that has been broken or wounded.
46. I bind and cast out every spirit of rebellion or disobedience that may try to lead my children astray, and I release a spirit of obedience and submission to God's will.
47. I declare that my children will be vessels of honor, used by God to bring salvation, healing, and deliverance to others.

48. I rebuke every spirit of confusion or indecision that may try to cloud my children's minds, and I release divine clarity and wisdom over their lives.
49. I pray for divine protection over my children's friendships, that they may be surrounded by godly influences and positive peer relationships.
50. I declare that my children's destiny is secure in Christ, and nothing can separate them from the love of God. I thank You, Lord, for hearing and answering my prayers. In Jesus' mighty name, Amen.

Chapter 6

A Warrior Mom's Journey into the Court of Heaven: A Step-by-Step Guide

A mother's love for her children knows no bounds, and a Warrior Mom understands that her battle extends beyond the physical realm. When faced with challenges and concerns for her children, she can embark on a spiritual journey into the Court of Heaven to fight for their well-being, seeking divine intervention and protection. This step-by-step guide, supported by relevant Bible references, will help empower Warrior Moms in their pursuit of justice and breakthrough.

Step 1: Seek God's Presence and Guidance
Before entering the Court of Heaven, a Warrior Mom must align herself with God's will and seek His presence. Spend time in prayer, worship, and meditation, allowing the Holy Spirit to lead and guide your steps (Psalm 16:11, Psalm 119:105).

Prayer Declaration:
Heavenly Father, I seek your presence and guidance in this journey. Fill me with your Holy Spirit, leading me in wisdom and discernment. I surrender my plans and desires to you, knowing that you have the best path for my children. In Jesus' name, I receive your divine direction.

Step 2: Understand the Legal Framework

The Court of Heaven operates based on legal principles outlined in Scripture. Familiarize yourself with biblical concepts such as the authority of the believer (Luke 10:19), the power of the blood of Jesus (Revelation 12:11), and the role of intercession (1 Timothy 2:1-2).

Prayer Declaration:

Mighty God, I thank you for the authority you have given me as a believer. I declare that I operate in the power and authority of Jesus Christ. By the blood of Jesus, I stand firm against any spiritual opposition. I claim victory over every challenge and declare that your justice will prevail in my children's lives.

Step 3: Identify the Issue

Clearly identify the concerns or challenges you want to address on behalf of your children. Be specific in your prayers, petitions, and declarations, presenting your case before God with faith and confidence (Hebrews 4:16, Matthew 7:7-8).

Prayer Declaration:

Lord, I present before you the specific concerns I have for my children. I bring clarity and precision to my prayers, petitions, and declarations. I trust that you hear my cries and that you are attentive to my children's needs. I believe that you will intervene and bring forth breakthrough.

Step 4: Repentance and Forgiveness

Before approaching the Court of Heaven, it is essential to examine your heart and ensure there is no unconfessed sin or unforgiveness. Repentance and forgiveness pave the way for God's grace and favor to flow (Matthew 6:14-15, 1 John 1:9).

Prayer Declaration:

Gracious Father, I humbly come before you, examining my heart and acknowledging any areas of sin or unforgiveness. I repent and ask for your forgiveness, cleansing me from all unrighteousness. Help me to extend forgiveness to those who have wronged me, releasing any bitterness or resentment. I receive your grace to walk in forgiveness and experience the freedom it brings.

Step 5: Decree and Declare God's Promises

As a Warrior Mom, speak God's Word over your children's lives, declaring His promises and purposes. Use Scriptures relevant to your situation, such as Psalm 127:3, Proverbs 22:6, and Isaiah 54:13. Stand firm in faith, knowing that God's Word does not return void (Isaiah 55:11).

Prayer Declaration:

Faithful God, I declare your promises over my children's lives. I declare that they are fearfully and wonderfully made, destined for greatness. I declare that they will walk in wisdom and knowledge, guided by your Spirit. I declare that no weapon formed against them shall prosper, and they will fulfill the purposes you have for them. I trust in your Word, knowing that it is powerful and effective.

Step 6: Engage in Spiritual Warfare
Recognize that your battle is not against flesh and blood but against spiritual forces (Ephesians 6:12). Put on the full armor of God, including the belt of truth, the breastplate of righteousness, the shield of faith, the helmet of salvation, the sword of the Spirit, and the readiness of the gospel of peace (Ephesians 6:13-18).

Prayer Declaration:
Mighty God, I put on the full armor of God to engage in spiritual warfare on behalf of my children. I gird myself with the belt of truth, knowing that your Word is the ultimate truth. I put on the breastplate of righteousness, guarding their hearts and minds. I take up the shield of faith to extinguish all fiery darts of the enemy. I place the helmet of salvation on their heads, securing their identity in Christ. I wield the sword of the Spirit, which is your Word, speaking it with authority against every spiritual attack. I stand firm and declare victory in Jesus' name.

Step 7: Present Your Case in the Court of Heaven
Approach the Court of Heaven with humility and reverence, acknowledging God as the ultimate Judge (Psalm 50:6). In prayer, present your case, pleading the blood of Jesus, and asking for divine intervention and justice (Revelation 12:11, Hebrews 12:24).

Prayer Declaration:

Heavenly Judge, I come before your throne of grace with humility and reverence. I present my case concerning my children, pleading the blood of Jesus over them. I declare that your justice and righteousness prevail. I ask for your divine intervention, protection, and breakthrough in their lives. Let your will be done, and let your kingdom come in their circumstances. I trust in your perfect judgment and believe that you will grant the desired outcome according to your wisdom.

Step 8: Activate Angelic Assistance

Invoke God's angelic hosts to fight alongside you. Declare angelic assignments in alignment with God's will and purpose, calling upon angelic protection and intervention on behalf of your children (Psalm 91:11-12, Hebrews 1:14).

Prayer Declaration:

Lord of Hosts, I call upon your angelic hosts to fight alongside me on behalf of my children. I declare that angels are encamped around them, providing protection and guidance. I command angelic assignments to be activated in alignment with your will and purpose. Let your angels guard them against every scheme of the enemy. Thank you for the heavenly reinforcements that surround my children day and night.

Step 9: Trust in God's Timing and Sovereignty

After presenting your case, trust in God's timing and sovereignty. Understand that His ways are higher than ours and that He works all things together for the good of those who love Him (Romans 8:28, Ecclesiastes 3:11).

Prayer Declaration:
Faithful Father, I surrender my timeline and desires to your perfect timing and sovereignty. I acknowledge that your ways are higher than mine, and your thoughts are beyond my comprehension. I trust that you are working all things together for the good of my children. I rest in the assurance that you hold their future in your hands. I choose to walk in faith, knowing that you are faithful to fulfill your promises.

Step 10: Walk in Faith and Obedience
Continue to stand in faith, believing that God is at work on behalf of your children. Walk in obedience to His Word and promptings, trusting that He will fulfill His promises and bring about the desired outcome (Hebrews 11:6, James 2:26).

Prayer Declaration:
Lord, I commit to walking in faith and obedience as I continue this journey on behalf of my children. I choose to trust your guidance and follow your leading. Strengthen me in moments of doubt or discouragement. Help me to align my actions with your Word and live a life that honors you. I believe that as I walk in faith and obedience, you will bring about the desired outcomes for my children. In Jesus' name, I declare that their lives are transformed and blessed by your grace.

A Warrior Mom's journey into the Court of Heaven is a powerful expression of love, faith, and perseverance. By following this step-by-step guide and anchoring your actions in biblical principles, you can fight for your children in the spiritual realm, trusting that God will bring about justice, protection, and breakthrough. Remember, as you embark on this journey, God is with you every step of the way (Isaiah 41:10).

"Pray in the language of heaven (Pray in tongues) for at least 10 minutes as you enter into the court of heaven to plead you case; if you cannot pray in tongues, enter His court with praise and worship for at least 10 minutes before you plead your case."

Warfare Prayers:

1. In the name of Jesus, I declare that I am a Warrior Mom, empowered by the Holy Spirit to fight for my children's well-being and protection.
2. I decree and declare that my children are covered by the blood of Jesus, and no weapon formed against them shall prosper.
3. I bind and rebuke every spirit of fear, doubt, and confusion that seeks to hinder my prayers and faith for my children.
4. I declare that my children are surrounded by a hedge of angelic protection, and no harm shall come near them.

5. I release the power of God's Word over my children's lives, speaking life, blessings, and divine favor into their present and future.
6. I break every generational curse or negative pattern that may affect my children's lives, declaring freedom and restoration in Jesus' name.
7. I declare that my children walk in divine health and wholeness, and every sickness or infirmity is eradicated from their bodies.
8. I declare that my children are filled with wisdom, knowledge, and understanding, and they excel academically, spiritually, and emotionally.
9. I bind the spirit of rebellion and disobedience in my children, declaring that they have a heart of submission and honor towards God and authority.
10. I decree and declare that my children are protected from the influence of negative peer pressure, and they choose godly friendships and associations.
11. I cancel every assignment of the enemy to steal, kill, or destroy the destiny and purpose of my children. They walk in their God-given calling and fulfill their divine assignments.
12. I declare that my children have a hunger and thirst for righteousness, and they pursue a deep relationship with God throughout their lives.
13. I bind and cast out any demonic influence or addiction that may try to entangle my children, declaring their freedom and deliverance in Jesus' name.

14. I declare that my children have a heart of gratitude and humility, and they walk in gratitude for God's blessings and goodness in their lives.
15. I decree and declare that my children have a spirit of discernment, and they can distinguish between good and evil, making wise choices in every situation.
16. I command every negative word spoken against my children's lives to be null and void. I release the power of God's Word to counteract every negative declaration.
17. I declare that my children are filled with the fruit of the Holy Spirit—love, joy, peace, patience, kindness, goodness, faithfulness, gentleness, and self-control.
18. I bind and break any curse or assignment of failure or lack over my children's lives, declaring that they walk in abundance and prosperity in all areas.
19. I pray for divine connections and opportunities for my children, that they may be surrounded by mentors and influencers who guide them in their journey.
20. I declare that my children are blessed in their going out and coming in. They are the head and not the tail, above and not beneath.
21. I plead the blood of Jesus over my children's minds, protecting them from negative thoughts, mental attacks, and the influence of worldly philosophies.

22. I declare that my children are vessels of God's love and compassion, impacting their communities and bringing transformation wherever they go.
23. I bind the spirit of rebellion and prodigality, declaring that my children will always return to their heavenly Father's embrace and walk in righteousness.
24. I break every chain of addiction, bondage, and destructive habits in my children's lives, declaring their freedom and victory in Jesus' name.
25. I declare that my children are anointed and appointed for such a time as this, and they will rise up as leaders and influencers in their generation.
26. I cancel every plan or assignment of the enemy to sow seeds of division or strife among my children. They walk in unity, love, and harmony.
27. I release the power of forgiveness in my children's lives, declaring that they have the grace to forgive others and receive forgiveness for themselves.
28. I declare divine protection over my children's relationships, guarding them from toxic or abusive connections and guiding them to healthy and God-centered friendships.
29. I pray for my children's spiritual eyes to be opened, that they may see the reality of the spiritual realm and discern the schemes of the enemy.

30. I declare that my children have a heart of worship and intimacy with God, cultivating a lifestyle of prayer, praise, and devotion to Him.
31. I break every chain of fear and anxiety in my children's lives, declaring that they walk in peace that surpasses all understanding.
32. I declare that my children have a heart of gratitude for their salvation, never taking for granted the sacrifice of Jesus on the cross.
33. I declare that my children have a heart of generosity, stewarding their resources to bless others and advance God's kingdom on earth.
34. I bind and cast out any spirit of rebellion or disobedience in my children, declaring their submission to God's authority and guidance.
35. I release the power of God's love over my children, declaring that they experience His unconditional love and acceptance in every season of their lives.
36. I declare that my children have a strong identity in Christ, knowing who they are and whose they are, and they walk in confidence and purpose.
37. I pray for divine wisdom and discernment to guide my parenting journey, that I may be an effective and godly parent to my children.
38. I declare that my children are protected from accidents, dangers, and any form of harm. Your angels surround them, Lord, keeping them safe.

39. I declare that my children have a heart of purity and holiness, guarding their minds and hearts from the influence of impurity and immorality.
40. I decree and declare that my children have a spirit of excellence, pursuing excellence in all areas of their lives for the glory of God.
41. I pray for divine opportunities and open doors for my children's dreams and aspirations, that they may walk in the fullness of their potential.
42. I declare that my children have a heart of forgiveness, releasing others from any offenses and experiencing the freedom that forgiveness brings.
43. I break every stronghold of fear or timidity in my children's lives, declaring that they walk in boldness and confidence to share their faith.
44. I declare that my children are filled with God's peace that transcends circumstances, calming their hearts and minds in every situation.
45. I bind and cast out any spirit of addiction or dependency in my children's lives, declaring their freedom and deliverance by the power of Jesus' name.
46. I declare that my children are instruments of healing and reconciliation, bringing restoration and unity wherever they go.
47. I pray for divine protection over my children's emotions, shielding them from depression, anxiety, and any form of emotional distress.

48. I declare that my children have a heart of gratitude for the blessings and provision of God, cultivating a lifestyle of thanksgiving.
49. I release the power of God's promises over my children's lives, declaring that they will fulfill their God-given destinies and walk in their calling.
50. I declare that my children are overcomers by the blood of the Lamb and the word of their testimony. They are victorious in every battle and circumstance.

Chapter 7

Your Child's Defender: Intercessory Prayer Principles

As a Warrior Mom, one of your most potent weapons in the spiritual battle for your children is intercessory prayer. You stand in the gap for your children, advocating for them before God and against the forces of darkness. This chapter delves deep into the principles of intercessory prayer, equipping you with the knowledge and understanding to be an effective intercessor.

Intercessory prayer is not ordinary prayer; it is a form of spiritual warfare. Intercession means standing between, taking up the case of another. In spiritual terms, it means coming before God on behalf of your children, pleading their case, praying for their needs, their protection, their growth, and their destiny.

The first principle of intercessory prayer is the recognition of your role as an intercessor. This role is not just about praying; it's about standing in the gap, fighting in the spirit, and defending your children in the spiritual realm. As a Warrior Mom, you are a defender, a guardian, a spiritual watchman over your children. Recognize this role, embrace it, and step into it with confidence and authority.

The second principle is understanding the power of prayer. Prayer is not a religious ritual; it's a spiritual weapon. It's not about saying the right words; it's about releasing God's power and will into a situation. James 5:16 says, "The prayer of a righteous person is powerful and effective." Your prayers as a mom carry power, and they produce results. Don't underestimate the power of your prayers. Each prayer is like a spiritual seed that you sow into the lives of your children, and it will bear fruit in due time.

The third principle of intercessory prayer is praying according to God's will. 1 John 5:14-15 tells us, "This is the confidence we have in approaching God: that if we ask anything according to His will, He hears us. And if we know that He hears us—whatever we ask—we know that we have what we asked of Him." Praying according to God's will means aligning our prayers with God's Word and His plans and purposes. It means praying not just what we want for our children but what God wants for them.

The fourth principle is persistency in prayer. Intercessory prayer is not a one-time event; it's a lifestyle. It requires perseverance, persistence, and patience. Jesus, in Luke 18:1-8, told a parable encouraging us always to pray and not give up. Persistent prayer doesn't mean we're trying to convince a reluctant God; it means we're pushing back the forces of darkness, enforcing God's will, and releasing His power into our children's lives.

The fifth principle of intercessory prayer is faith. Hebrews 11:6 says, "Without faith, it is impossible to please God..." When we pray, we must believe that God hears us and that He will answer us. We must have faith in God's power, His promises, and His faithfulness. Our faith is not in the intensity of our prayers, the eloquence of our words, or the length of our prayer sessions; our faith is in God.

The sixth principle is the use of the Word of God in our prayers. Ephesians 6:17 describes the Word of God as the sword of the Spirit. As we pray God's Word, we are wielding a spiritual weapon, cutting through lies, demolishing strongholds, and establishing truth. When you pray God's promises over your children, you're not just wishing good things for them; you're enforcing God's will in their lives.

The seventh principle is praying in the Spirit. Romans 8:26-27 tells us that the Holy Spirit helps us in our weakness and intercedes for us according to God's will. Praying in the Spirit can mean praying in tongues, but it also means allowing the Holy Spirit to guide our prayers, praying with the heart and mind of the Spirit.

Intercessory prayer is a high calling and a mighty weapon. As a Warrior Mom, your prayers carry power, they make a difference, and they defend your children in the spiritual realm. It's not just about praying; it's about fighting, standing in the gap, and wielding spiritual weapons for the victory of your children. As you grow in understanding and applying these principles, you become not just a praying mom, but a Warrior Mom, standing in the gap and defending your children in the court of heaven.

"Pray in the language of heaven (Pray in tongues) for at least 10 minutes as you enter into the court of heaven to plead you case; if you cannot pray in tongues, enter His court with praise and worship for at least 10 minutes before you plead your case."

Warfare Prayers:

1. In the name of Jesus, I declare that my child is covered by the blood of the Lamb, and no weapon formed against them shall prosper.
2. I proclaim that my child is surrounded by a hedge of divine protection, and every plan of the enemy concerning their life is nullified.
3. Heavenly Father, I declare that my child walks in the light of your truth, and no darkness can prevail against them.
4. I rebuke every spirit of fear, anxiety, and confusion that tries to torment my child. I declare peace and soundness of mind over them.
5. I bind every spirit of rebellion and disobedience that may try to influence my child. I declare that they have a heart of obedience and submission to God.

6. I break every generational curse and negative pattern in my child's life. I declare freedom and breakthrough in every area.
7. Lord, I pray that my child will be filled with the Holy Spirit and operate in the gifts and fruit of the Spirit for their divine purpose.
8. I come against any sickness, disease, or infirmity that may try to attack my child's body. I declare divine health and vitality over them.
9. I declare that my child is a vessel of God's love, spreading kindness, compassion, and forgiveness wherever they go.
10. I bind every negative influence from peers and the media that may try to sway my child from the path of righteousness.
11. I pray for godly friendships and mentors to be established in my child's life, guiding them in wisdom and truth.
12. I declare that my child's mind is protected from the lies and deception of the enemy. Their thoughts are aligned with God's Word.
13. I plead the blood of Jesus over my child's relationships, that they will experience healthy, nurturing connections with others.
14. I declare supernatural wisdom and discernment for my child, enabling them to make godly choices and avoid pitfalls.
15. I pray for divine favor and open doors for my child's education, talents, and future endeavors. Their gifts will be used for God's glory.
16. I come against any addiction or bondage that may try to entangle my child. I declare freedom and deliverance in the name of Jesus.

17. I declare that my child is a world changer, a light in the darkness, and an instrument of God's peace wherever they go.
18. I pray for angelic protection around my child, that they will be guarded from any harm or danger.
19. I break every curse of failure and mediocrity over my child's life. I declare success and excellence in all their endeavors.
20. I release a spirit of perseverance and resilience upon my child, that they will overcome challenges and rise above adversity.
21. I declare that my child's identity is firmly rooted in Christ. They will not be swayed by the opinions of others but stand firm in their faith.
22. I bind the spirit of rebellion and prodigality. I declare that my child will come to their senses and return to the loving arms of the Father.
23. I pray for divine opportunities for my child to share their faith and be a witness to others. They will boldly proclaim the gospel.
24. I declare that my child's future is secure in God's hands. Their steps are ordered by the Lord, and they will fulfill their destiny.
25. Finally, I thank you, Lord, for hearing my prayers and for being faithful to watch over my child. I trust in your promises and declare victory in every battle. Amen.

Chapter 8

The Power of a Mother's Prayer: The Art of Petitioning

A mother's prayer carries a unique weight and intensity. It rises from a heart brimming with love and concern for her children, making it a potent force in the spiritual realm. This chapter unravels the art of petitioning - a form of prayer that is all about making specific requests known to God, outlining the power of a mother's prayer, and guiding you, the Warrior Mom, to wield this weapon effectively.

The word 'petition' in its original Latin means 'to seek, go to, beg, strive after.' To petition God, then, is to earnestly seek Him, laying before Him the desires of our hearts, striving after His will. Petitioning is a form of prayer that includes specific requests, direct pleas to God for your children's spiritual, emotional, physical, and future needs.

The first principle of the art of petitioning is to pray with specificity. Rather than generic prayers, bring specific requests before God. Pray for your child's future spouse, their career path, their friendships, their spiritual growth, their struggles, and their dreams. Specific prayers allow us to see specific answers and thus increase our faith.

The second principle is praying with faith. When you petition God, you must do so believing that He hears you and will answer. The Bible says in Mark 11:24, "Therefore I tell you, whatever you ask in prayer, believe that you have received it, and it will be yours." Your faith is not in the outcome you desire but in God who is sovereign and who has your children's best interests at heart.

The third principle is praying with persistence. Petitioning is not a hit-or-miss endeavor; it involves consistent, persistent prayer. Jesus Himself taught us to persist in prayer through the parable of the persistent widow (Luke 18:1-8). God is not annoyed by our persistent prayers; instead, He is moved by our faith and perseverance.

The fourth principle is praying in alignment with God's will. This is where the knowledge of God's Word becomes crucial. As you understand God's heart revealed through Scripture, you can align your petitions with His will. For instance, you know it is God's will for your children to be saved (2 Peter 3:9), to be sanctified (1 Thessalonians 4:3), and to serve others (Galatians 5:13). Therefore, you can pray confidently, knowing your petitions align with God's purposes.

The fifth principle is praying with expectancy. Petitioning involves not just presenting our requests to God but also expecting Him to answer. This expectancy is not a demand but a confident hope in God's faithfulness. Psalm 5:3 says, "In the morning, LORD, you hear my voice; in the morning I lay my requests before you and wait expectantly."

The sixth principle is praying with surrender. While we bring our specific requests to God, we also acknowledge His sovereignty. We surrender our desires, our plans, our expectations to His wisdom and timing. It's trusting that even if His answers are not what we expected, they are always what's best for our children.

The power of a mother's prayer is not based on her eloquence, her piety, or her persistence; it is rooted in the One to whom she prays. God hears, He cares, and He answers. Your role as a Warrior Mom is to lift your voice, make your petitions known, and trust that God is at work.

As you grow in the art of petitioning, remember that it's not just about getting what you want for your children. It's about engaging with God, aligning your heart with His, and becoming a conduit of His power and purposes for your children. It's about standing as a Warrior Mom, wielding the weapon of prayer, and defending your children in the court of heaven.

> ***"Pray in the language of heaven (Pray in tongues) for at least 10 minutes as you enter into the court of heaven to plead you case; if you cannot pray in tongues, enter His court with praise and worship for at least 10 minutes before you plead your case."***

Warfare Prayers:

1. Heavenly Father, I declare that my children are surrounded by your divine protection. No weapon formed against them shall prosper, and every tongue that rises against them in judgment will be condemned. (Isaiah 54:17)
2. Lord, I break and nullify every generational curse and stronghold that may have been passed down to my children. I declare freedom and deliverance over their lives in the mighty name of Jesus.
3. I declare that my children walk in wisdom and discernment. I pray that they make godly choices and are led by the Holy Spirit in every decision they make.
4. Father, I pray against any spirit of fear or anxiety that may try to torment my children. I declare peace and soundness of mind over them, for you have not given them a spirit of fear but of power, love, and a sound mind. (2 Timothy 1:7)
5. I declare that my children are overcomers. They have victory over every trial and temptation they face because greater is He who is in them than he who is in the world. (1 John 4:4)
6. Lord, I pray for divine health and protection over my children. I declare that they are covered by the blood of Jesus, and no sickness or disease shall come near them. (Psalm 91:10)
7. I declare that my children excel academically. They have a spirit of excellence and are diligent in their studies. I pray for favor with their teachers and peers.
8. Father, I declare that my children have a heart for you. They love you with all their heart, soul, and mind, and they walk in obedience to your Word.

9. I pray against any negative influence or ungodly friendships in my children's lives. I declare that they are surrounded by godly friends who will encourage and support them in their faith.
10. Lord, I declare that my children are filled with the Holy Spirit. I pray that they operate in the gifts of the Spirit and are used by you to bring glory to your name.
11. I bind and rebuke any spirit of rebellion or disobedience that may try to influence my children. I declare that they have a heart that submits to authority and walks in humility.
12. Father, I declare that my children have a heart for justice and righteousness. They stand up for the oppressed and make a positive impact in their communities.
13. I pray for divine guidance and direction in my children's lives. I declare that they walk in the path that you have set before them and fulfill the purpose you have for them.
14. Lord, I pray for emotional healing and restoration for my children. I declare that any past wounds or hurts are healed by the power of your love and grace.
15. I declare that my children have a hunger for your Word. They study and meditate on it day and night, and it is a lamp unto their feet and a light unto their path. (Psalm 119:105)
16. Father, I pray for divine favor and open doors of opportunity for my children. I declare that they walk in the favor of God in every area of their lives.

17. I pray against any addiction or bondage in my children's lives. I declare freedom and deliverance from every chain that may try to hold them captive.
18. Lord, I declare that my children have a heart of gratitude and thankfulness. They acknowledge you in all their ways, and you direct their paths. (Proverbs 3:6)
19. I pray for divine protection over my children's minds. I declare that they have the mind of Christ, and every thought is taken captive to the obedience of Christ. (2 Corinthians 10:5)
20. Father, I pray for godly mentors and role models in my children's lives. I declare that they are surrounded by men and women of faith who will guide and encourage them.
21. I declare that my children have a heart for missions and spreading the Gospel. They have a burden for the lost and boldly share the love of Christ wherever they go.
22. Lord, I pray for divine provision in every area of my children's lives. I declare that you supply all their needs according to your riches in glory by Christ Jesus. (Philippians 4:19)
23. I pray against any spirit of complacency or lukewarmness in my children's spiritual lives. I declare that they are on fire for you, Lord, and their passion for you only grows stronger.
24. Father, I declare that my children have a heart of forgiveness and love. They forgive others as you have forgiven them, and they love others unconditionally.

25. I pray for a hedge of angels to surround my children, guarding and protecting them from all harm. I declare that they are safe and secure in your hands, Lord.

Chapter 9

Warrior Mom:
Unleashing Divine Power for Your Children's Protection

A warrior mom is a powerful force of love, protection, and guidance in her children's lives. She recognizes the responsibility she has to nurture and safeguard her children, and she taps into divine power to strengthen and equip herself for this sacred task. Through prayer, faith, and the guidance of Scripture, a warrior mom can unleash divine power for her children's protection.

Prayer is a vital tool for a warrior mom. It is through prayer that she connects with God, expressing her concerns, fears, and hopes for her children. In Matthew 21:22, Jesus said, "And whatever you ask in prayer, you will receive if you have faith." A warrior mom's prayers are filled with faith, believing that God hears her and is actively working in her children's lives. She prays for their safety, health, wisdom, and spiritual growth. Through prayer, she invites God's divine protection into their lives, trusting that He will watch over them.

A warrior mom also finds strength and guidance in the Word of God. The Bible provides wisdom, comfort, and promises to cling to during challenging times. In Psalm 91:4, it says, "He will cover you with his feathers, and under his wings, you will find refuge." This verse reminds a warrior mom that God is a shelter and a shield for her children. She meditates on Scriptures that speak of God's faithfulness, love, and protection, such as Psalm 121:7-8, which states, "The Lord will keep you from all harm—he will watch over your life; the Lord will watch over your coming and going both now and forevermore."

A warrior mom also understands the importance of nurturing her children's faith. Proverbs 22:6 instructs, "Train up a child in the way he should go; even when he is old, he will not depart from it." By teaching her children about God's love, grace, and truth, she equips them to navigate life's challenges with a solid foundation. She encourages them to develop their relationship with God, guiding them in prayer, Bible study, and involvement in a faith community. By instilling godly values and principles, a warrior mom empowers her children to make wise choices and stay grounded in their faith.

Furthermore, a warrior mom recognizes the significance of her own spiritual growth. She understands that she cannot pour from an empty cup. She carves out time for personal prayer, reflection, and study of the Bible. She seeks the guidance of the Holy Spirit to shape her character, helping her become a better example and guide for her children. Galatians 5:22-23 reminds her of the fruit of the Spirit, saying, "But the fruit of the Spirit is love, joy, peace, forbearance, kindness, goodness, faithfulness, gentleness, and self-control." These qualities are essential in her role as a warrior mom, as they create a nurturing and loving environment for her children.

A warrior mom unleashes divine power for her children's protection through prayer, faith, and the guidance of Scripture. By consistently seeking God's presence, she taps into His strength and wisdom to fulfill her role as a loving and protective parent. She trusts in His promises, finds comfort in His Word, and guides her children towards a deep and meaningful relationship with God. As she embraces her calling as a warrior mom, she becomes a powerful instrument of divine protection and love in her children's lives.

She is deeply devoted to her children and their well-being, engages in intercession and prayer as a means to protect and support them. Through her prayers, she actively seeks divine intervention and guidance from God, aiming to shield her children from harm and ensure their safety. Here's a breakdown of how a warrior mom intercedes on behalf of her children and forges a spiritual shield around them:

Faith and Trust:

A warrior mom's intercession begins with a strong foundation of faith and trust in God's power and love. She believes that God is always present, caring for her children, and is willing to respond to her prayers.

Declaration of Protection:

I declare that my children are divinely protected by the Almighty God. No weapon formed against them shall prosper, and every tongue that rises against them in judgment shall be condemned (Isaiah 54:17).

Declaration of Guidance:
I declare that God's perfect guidance is upon my children. He will instruct them and teach them in the way they should go; He will counsel them with His loving eye upon them (Psalm 32:8).

Declaration of Provision:
I declare that my children will lack no good thing, for the Lord is their shepherd. He will lead them beside still waters and restore their souls. They shall dwell in His abundance all the days of their lives (Psalm 23:1, 2, 6).

Declaration of Healing:
I declare divine health and healing over my children's bodies. By the stripes of Jesus, they are healed from all infirmities, diseases, and sicknesses. They walk in the fullness of God's healing power (Isaiah 53:5; 1 Peter 2:24).

Declaration of Favor:
I declare that my children are highly favored by God and by people. They will find favor and good understanding in the sight of God and all those they come in contact with. God's favor will open doors of opportunities for them (Luke 2:52; Proverbs 3:4).

Praying for Protection:

A key aspect of intercession for a warrior mom is praying specifically for protection for her children. She acknowledges that there are unseen dangers and challenges in the world and asks God to shield her children from harm.

Declaration of God's Angelic Protection:
Heavenly Father, I declare your promise of angelic protection over my life. Your Word in Psalm 91:11 says, 'For he will command his angels concerning you to guard you in all your ways.' I believe that your angels are encamped around me, shielding me from unseen dangers and challenges. I trust in your divine protection and thank you for your faithfulness. Amen.

Declaration of God's Shield of Favor:
Gracious Lord, I declare your shield of favor to surround me, shielding me from every unseen danger and challenge. Your Word in Psalm 5:12 assures me, 'For you bless the righteous, O Lord; you cover him with favor as with a shield.' I receive your favor and protection, knowing that you are with me wherever I go. Thank you for being my refuge and stronghold. Amen.

Declaration of God's Armor of Protection:
Mighty God, I put on the full armor of God, as described in Ephesians 6:10-18, to protect me from unseen dangers and challenges. I declare that

I am covered by the belt of truth, the breastplate of righteousness, the shoes of the gospel of peace, the shield of faith, the helmet of salvation, and the sword of the Spirit, which is the Word of God. With this armor, I stand strong against all spiritual attacks, knowing that victory is mine in Christ. Amen.

Declaration of God's Deliverance from Evil:
Heavenly Father, I declare your deliverance from all unseen dangers and challenges that come against me. Your Word in 2 Thessalonians 3:3 assures me, 'But the Lord is faithful. He will establish you and guard you against the evil one.' I trust in your faithfulness to protect me and keep me safe from every harm. Thank you for your unfailing love and your constant watchfulness over me. Amen.

Declaration of God's Peace in the Midst of Storms:
Prince of Peace, I declare your peace to reign in my life, even in the face of unseen dangers and challenges. Your Word in Philippians 4:7 says, 'And the peace of God, which surpasses all understanding, will guard your hearts and your minds in Christ Jesus.' I receive your peace that surpasses understanding, knowing that it will guard my heart and mind from fear, worry, and anxiety. I trust in your abiding presence and your calming peace. Amen.

Spiritual Armor:

The warrior mom may visualize her prayers as a spiritual armor enveloping her children. This armor serves as a shield against negative influences, temptations, and any forces that could potentially harm her children physically, emotionally, or spiritually.

Prayer Declarations

Heavenly Father, I declare your powerful protection over my children, shielding them from negative influences and temptations. In the name of Jesus, I pray that you surround them with your divine presence, guarding them against any harm. "But the Lord is faithful. He will establish you and guard you against the evil one" (2 Thessalonians 3:3).

Lord, I declare that no weapon formed against my children shall prosper. I plead the blood of Jesus over them, covering them from any physical, emotional, or spiritual harm. "No weapon that is fashioned against you shall succeed, and you shall refute every tongue that rises against you in judgment" (Isaiah 54:17).

Gracious God, I declare that my children are kept safe from the snares of the enemy. I pray that you set a hedge of protection around them, so that no evil can penetrate their lives. "He will cover you with his pinions, and under his wings you will find refuge; his faithfulness is a shield and buckler" (Psalm 91:4).

Heavenly Father, I declare that my children are surrounded by your angels, who excel in strength, to watch over them day and night. I thank you for dispatching your heavenly host to safeguard them from any danger. "For he will command his angels concerning you to guard you in all your ways" (Psalm 91:11).

Lord, I declare victory over any spiritual battle that my children may face. I pray that you equip them with the full armor of God, empowering them to stand firm against the schemes of the enemy. "Put on the whole armor of God, that you may be able to stand against the schemes of the devil" (Ephesians 6:11).

Releasing Divine Protection:

Through her prayers, the warrior mom releases her concerns and desires for her children into God's hands. She recognizes that God's divine protection surpasses her own abilities and trusts that He will watch over her children, guiding and guarding them in every situation.

Prayer Declarations

Heavenly Father, I release all my concerns and desires for my children into your capable hands, knowing that you love them even more than I do. I trust in your promise from Proverbs 22:6: "Train up a child in the way he should go; even when he is old he will not depart from it." I surrender their paths to you, believing that you will guide and protect them.

Almighty God, I surrender my anxieties and desires for my children's future into your sovereign control. I am reminded of your words in

Jeremiah 29:11: "For I know the plans I have for you, declares the Lord, plans for welfare and not for evil, to give you a future and a hope." I release my fears and ask you to lead my children according to your perfect plans for their lives.

Heavenly Father, I let go of any worries and desires I have for my children's well-being and safety. I stand on your promise from Psalm 91:11: "For he will command his angels concerning you to guard you in all your ways." I entrust my children's protection into your hands, knowing that you have assigned angels to watch over them and keep them safe from harm.

Lord, I release all my concerns and desires for my children's spiritual growth and relationship with you. I trust in your assurance from Philippians 1:6: "And I am sure of this, that he who began a good work in you will bring it to completion at the day of Jesus Christ." I surrender their spiritual journeys to you, believing that you will continue to work in their lives, drawing them closer to you and molding them into your image.

Almighty God, I declare that I surrender my desires for my children's success and achievements into your hands. I am reminded of your words in Psalm 37:5: "Commit your way to the Lord; trust in him, and he will act." I release any pressures and expectations, trusting that as my children commit their paths to you, you will guide them and bring about the best outcomes according to Your will.

Praying for Guidance:

Along with protection, a warrior mom intercedes for divine guidance for her children. She seeks wisdom, discernment, and clarity for them to make wise decisions, avoid harmful situations, and choose the right path in life.

Prayer Declarations

Heavenly Father, I declare that my children shall walk in the path of divine guidance. I pray that you will grant them wisdom, discernment, and clarity in every decision they make. Proverbs 3:5-6 says, "Trust in the Lord with all your heart and lean not on your own understanding; in all your ways submit to him, and he will make your paths straight." I trust that you will lead them on the right path and provide them with the discernment to make wise choices.

Lord, I declare that your Word will be a lamp unto my children's feet and a light unto their path. Psalm 119:105 says, "Your word is a lamp for my feet, a light on my path." I pray that as they meditate on your Word and seek your guidance, you will illuminate their way and give them clear direction in all areas of their lives.

Heavenly Father, I declare that my children will have the mind of Christ. 1 Corinthians 2:16 says, "But we have the mind of Christ." I pray that you will grant them wisdom beyond their years and a discerning spirit. Help them to make decisions that align with your will and purpose for their lives.

Lord, I declare that my children will listen and follow your voice. John 10:27 says, "My sheep listen to my voice; I know them, and they follow me." I pray that they will have sensitive hearts to hear your still small voice, and that they will have the courage and obedience to follow your leading. May they not be swayed by the opinions of others but be anchored in your truth.

Heavenly Father, I declare that my children will walk in clarity and understanding. Proverbs 4:7 says, "The beginning of wisdom is this: Get wisdom. Though it cost all you have, get understanding." I pray that you will grant them a deep understanding of your ways and purposes. Fill them with your Spirit of wisdom, so they may navigate life with clarity and discernment, making choices that honor and glorify you. In Jesus' name I pray, amen.

Trusting God's Plan:

While the warrior mom prays fervently for her children's protection, she also acknowledges that God has a greater plan for their lives. She surrenders control, understanding that sometimes challenges and difficulties are part of their growth and spiritual journey. She trusts that God will work all things together for their ultimate good.

Consistent Prayer:

A warrior mom's intercession is not a one-time event but a continuous practice. She establishes a regular prayer routine, lifting up her children daily, and remains persistent and faithful in her prayers.

Strengthening Spiritual Connection:

The warrior mom nurtures her own spiritual relationship with God through prayer, reading sacred texts, attending religious services, and seeking spiritual guidance. This connection deepens her ability to intercede effectively for her children.

Overall, a warrior mom's intercession on behalf of her children involves seeking God's protection, guidance, and blessings through prayer. Her commitment, faith, and love provide a powerful spiritual shield that surrounds her children, creating an atmosphere of divine intervention and safeguarding them from unseen dangers.

> *"Pray in the language of heaven (Pray in tongues) for at least 10 minutes as you enter into the court of heaven to plead you case; if you cannot pray in tongues, enter His court with praise and worship for at least 10 minutes before you plead your case."*

Warfare Prayers:

1. Heavenly Father, I come before your throne of grace, standing as a mother, interceding for my children's protection in the court of heaven. I plead the blood of Jesus over them as a covering against every power of darkness, witchcraft attack, and force of evil.
2. Lord, I declare that no weapon formed against my children shall prosper. I decree and declare divine immunity and supernatural protection over their lives.
3. In the name of Jesus, I dismantle every plan and assignment of the enemy targeted at my children. I bind and render null and void every demonic force that seeks to harm or influence them negatively.
4. Heavenly Father, surround my children with your mighty angels, creating a hedge of protection around them. Let your angelic hosts encamp around them day and night, thwarting every attack of the enemy.
5. I break and destroy every generational curse or evil pattern that has been operating in my family line, specifically targeting my children. I release them from the grip of any inherited spiritual attacks or witchcraft practices.
6. Lord, I pray for discernment and wisdom for my children to recognize and avoid any deceptive schemes of the enemy. Open their eyes to see the truth and protect them from any manipulation or coercion.
7. I command every curse, spell, or hex sent against my children to be nullified and returned to sender. Let every evil work be reversed, and let it have no lasting effect on their lives.

8. Heavenly Father, I pray for divine favor and divine connections for my children. Surround them with godly influences and protect them from negative peer pressure and harmful relationships.
9. I decree and declare that my children are hidden in the secret place of the Most High. They dwell under the shadow of your wings, and no evil shall befall them, nor any plague come near their dwelling.
10. Lord, I pray for a sound mind and emotional stability for my children. Protect them from any form of mental or emotional manipulation and heal any wounds or traumas they may have experienced.
11. I release the fire of God to consume every demonic altar or covenant that has been established against my children. Let every evil association be destroyed and let the power of darkness lose its grip over their lives.
12. I plead the blood of Jesus over their minds, that they may have clarity of thought, discernment, and divine understanding. Guard their thoughts and protect them from any spiritual contamination.
13. Lord, I pray for physical protection over my children. Shield them from accidents, illnesses, and any form of harm. Let divine health and vitality be their portion.
14. I declare that my children are overcomers by the blood of the Lamb and the word of their testimony. Strengthen them to resist every temptation and to stand firm in their faith against any attack.

15. Heavenly Father, I pray for supernatural breakthroughs in every area of my children's lives. Open doors that no man can shut and frustrate the plans of the enemy to hinder their progress.
16. I release the power of God's Word over my children. Let the truth of your Word be a lamp unto their feet and a light unto their path. Protect them from any false doctrine or deceptive teachings.
17. Lord, I pray for divine guidance and direction for my children. Lead them on the path of righteousness and protect them from making wrong choices or falling into dangerous situations.
18. I cancel and render powerless every word curse or negative declaration spoken against my children. I release the power of blessings and positive affirmations over their lives.
19. Heavenly Father, fill my children with your Holy Spirit. Let your Spirit empower them to resist the temptations of the world and to walk in holiness and purity.
20. Lord, I commit my children into your hands, knowing that you are their ultimate protector. I trust in your unfailing love and ask that you would always watch over them, keeping them safe from all harm.

Chapter 10

A Mother's Guide to Fighting for Her Children: Empowering Through Prayer on Bended Knees

As a mother, one of the most powerful tools you have in your arsenal when it comes to fighting for your children is prayer. When you kneel down in prayer, you humble yourself before God and surrender your worries, fears, and desires for your children into His hands. It is through prayer that you can seek strength, guidance, and protection for your little ones. The Bible encourages us to pray without ceasing and assures us that God hears our prayers. In Matthew 7:7, Jesus says, "Ask, and it will be given to you; seek, and you will find; knock, and it will be opened to you." So, on your knees with a heart full of faith, bring your children before God and pour out your prayers for their well-being and success.

Scripture provides numerous examples of mothers who fought for their children through prayer. One such example is Hannah, the mother of Samuel. In her desperation to have a child, she went to the temple and poured out her heart to God, praying fervently for a son. God heard her prayer, and she eventually gave birth to Samuel, who grew up to be a great prophet and leader in Israel. Hannah's story in 1 Samuel 1:10-20 reminds us that God is attentive to the cries of a mother's heart and that He can work miracles in the lives of our children when we seek Him with faith and persistence.

Prayer not only empowers you as a mother but also strengthens the bond between you and your children. When you pray for your children, you are inviting God to intervene in their lives, protect them from harm, and guide them in their decisions. You are acknowledging your dependence on God and teaching your children to trust in Him as well. Proverbs 22:6 instructs, "Train up a child in the way he should go; even when he is old, he will not depart from it." By praying for your children, you are instilling in them a foundation of faith and teaching them the value of seeking God in all aspects of life.

A mother's guide to fighting for her children on her knees with prayer is a powerful and effective approach. By humbling yourself before God and lifting your children up in prayer, you are inviting divine intervention into their lives. Remember the words of James 5:16, which says, "The prayer of a righteous person has great power as it is working." So, as you seek God's guidance and protection for your children, trust that He will hear your prayers and work mightily on their behalf.

Step-by-step Guide:

Start by surrendering your children to God:

Surrendering your children to God means acknowledging that He is ultimately in control and entrusting their lives to Him. It requires letting go of the need to control every outcome and trusting that God has a perfect plan for your children. By committing your children to the Lord, you are acknowledging His sovereignty and inviting Him to work in their lives for their ultimate good.

Heavenly Father, I surrender my children into your hands, trusting in your perfect plan for their lives. I declare Proverbs 22:6 over them, believing that as I train them in the way they should go, they will not depart from it.

Lord, I declare Psalm 127:3-4, acknowledging that my children are a heritage from you. I surrender them to you, recognizing that they are in your loving care, and I trust you to guide and protect them according to Your will.

Mighty God, I declare Isaiah 54:13, believing that my children will be taught by you and will experience great peace and prosperity in their lives. I surrender their education, friendships, and every aspect of their growth to your divine guidance and wisdom.

Lord Jesus, I surrender my children's health and well-being into your hands. I declare Psalm 103:2-3, affirming that you heal all their diseases and redeem their lives from destruction. I trust you to guard and nurture their physical, emotional, and spiritual well-being.

Gracious Father, I surrender my children's future and their destinies to you. I declare Jeremiah 29:11, knowing that you have plans to prosper them and give them hope and a future. I release any anxiety or fear and place my confidence in your sovereign and loving purposes for their lives.

Pray for wisdom and guidance:

As a mother, you face countless decisions and challenges regarding your children. Praying for wisdom and guidance invites God to provide insight and direction. The Bible assures us that if we lack wisdom, we can ask God, and He will generously give it to us. By seeking His guidance, you can make decisions that align with His will and best interests for your children.

Heavenly Father, I declare that you will grant me wisdom and guidance as a mother, helping me make decisions that align with your perfect will for my children. Your Word assures me in James 1:5, "If any of you lacks wisdom, you should ask God, who gives generously to all without finding fault, and it will be given to you."

Lord, I proclaim that you will grant me insight and discernment as I navigate the challenges of parenting. May your Spirit enlighten my mind and heart, enabling me to make choices that nurture and protect my children. Proverbs 2:6 reminds me, "For the Lord gives wisdom; from his mouth come knowledge and understanding."

Father, I declare that you will provide me with divine direction as I seek to lead my children on the right path. Psalm 32:8 assures me, "I will instruct you and teach you in the way you should go; I will counsel you with my loving eye on you." Grant me the clarity to guide my children according to your purpose for their lives.

Lord, I proclaim that you will grant me discernment to distinguish between good and evil, guiding me in making choices that promote righteousness and protect my children from harm. Hebrews 5:14 encourages me, "But solid food is for the mature, who by constant use have trained themselves to distinguish good from evil."

Heavenly Father, I declare that you will grant me divine wisdom in nurturing my children's faith and character. Help me instill in them a love for your Word and a heart that seeks after you. Proverbs 22:6 reminds me, "Start children off on the way they should go, and even when they are old they will not turn from it." Grant me the insight to cultivate their spiritual growth.

Seek God's protection over your children:

Every parent desire their children to be safe from harm. Praying for God's protection acknowledges that He is the ultimate guardian. By entrusting your children's safety to Him, you recognize His power to shield them from physical and spiritual dangers. Remember the promise in Psalm

121:7, which assures us that the Lord will keep us from all evil and protect our lives.

Declaration of God's Protection:
Heavenly Father, I declare your divine protection over my children. I trust in your promise to shield them from physical and spiritual dangers. I thank you for surrounding them with your angels and keeping them safe under your wings.
Scripture Reference: Psalm 91:11-12 - "For he will command his angels concerning you to guard you in all your ways. On their hands they will bear you up, lest you strike your foot against a stone."

Declaration of God's Presence:
Lord, I declare that your presence goes before my children wherever they go. May they always be aware of your nearness, knowing that you are with them in every situation. Keep them from harm and lead them into your perfect will.
Scripture Reference: Joshua 1:9 - "Have I not commanded you? Be strong and courageous. Do not be frightened, and do not be dismayed, for the Lord your God is with you wherever you go."

Declaration of Spiritual Armor:
Heavenly Father, I declare that my children are equipped with the full armor of God. Cover them with the belt of truth, breastplate of righteousness, shoes of the gospel of peace, shield of faith, helmet of

salvation, and the sword of the Spirit. May they stand firm against all spiritual attacks.

Scripture Reference: Ephesians 6:13-17 - "Therefore take up the whole armor of God, that you may be able to withstand in the evil day, and having done all, to stand firm. Stand therefore, having fastened on the belt of truth, and having put on the breastplate of righteousness, and, as shoes for your feet, having put on the readiness given by the gospel of peace. In all circumstances take up the shield of faith, with which you can extinguish all the flaming darts of the evil one; and take the helmet of salvation, and the sword of the Spirit, which is the word of God."

Declaration of Divine Guidance:

Lord, I declare that you will guide my children's steps and lead them away from danger. Surround them with your wisdom and discernment, helping them make right choices and avoiding harmful influences. May your Holy Spirit be their constant guide.

Scripture Reference: Proverbs 3:5-6 - "Trust in the Lord with all your heart, and do not lean on your own understanding. In all your ways acknowledge him, and he will make straight your paths."

Declaration of Deliverance:

Heavenly Father, I declare your deliverance over my children. Break every chain that seeks to bind them and set them free from every snare of the enemy. Protect them from the schemes of darkness and grant them victory over every spiritual battle they face.

Scripture Reference: Psalm 34:17 - "When the righteous cry for help, the Lord hears and delivers them out of all their troubles."

Pray for your children's salvation:

The most vital aspect of your children's lives is their relationship with God. Praying for their salvation involves asking God to draw them close to Him, to reveal His love and truth to them, and to lead them to accept Jesus as their Savior. Acts 16:31 declares that belief in the Lord Jesus leads to salvation, not just for individuals but also for their households. Trust God's faithfulness to work in the hearts of your children.

Heavenly Father, I declare that my children shall experience a deep and genuine love for you and your Word. I pray that their hearts will be drawn to seek you diligently, just as the psalmist declared in Psalm 119:10: "With my whole heart I seek you; let me not wander from your commandments."

Lord, I declare that my children shall have a revelation of the truth and beauty of your salvation. May they understand the sacrifice of Jesus Christ on the cross and accept Him as their personal Lord and Savior. As it is written in Romans 10:9, "If you confess with your mouth that Jesus is Lord and believe in your heart that God raised him from the dead, you will be saved."

Almighty God, I declare that my children's minds will be protected from the lies and deceptions of the enemy. May they develop a discerning spirit, guided by your Word. I claim the promise of 2 Corinthians 10:5 over them, that "we destroy arguments and every lofty opinion raised against the knowledge of God and take every thought captive to obey Christ."

Heavenly Father, I declare that my children will be filled with a hunger for your Word. May they find joy and delight in studying and meditating on Scripture. As the psalmist proclaimed in Psalm 119:16, "I will delight in your statutes; I will not forget your word." Let this be their testimony as well.

Lord, I declare that my children shall be rooted and established in a vibrant and personal relationship with you. May they grow in faith and walk in obedience to your commands. I claim the promise of Colossians 2:6-7 over their lives: "Therefore, as you received Christ Jesus the Lord, so walk in him, rooted and built up in him and established in the faith, just as you were taught, abounding in thanksgiving."

Declare God's promises over your children:

The Bible is filled with promises from God that apply to every aspect of our lives, including our children. By declaring these promises over your children through prayer, you are speaking God's truth and power into their lives. Remember that all the promises of God find their fulfillment in Christ (2 Corinthians 1:20), so you can confidently claim these promises as you pray.

Declaration of Protection:

Heavenly Father, I declare your powerful protection over my children. Your Word says in Psalm 91:11, 'For he will command his angels concerning you to guard you in all your ways.' I trust in your promise, Lord, that no weapon formed against them shall prosper, as stated in Isaiah 54:17. I thank you for surrounding them with your divine shield of defense. In Jesus' name, amen.

Declaration of Wisdom:

Gracious Father, I declare your wisdom upon my children. Your Word assures us in James 1:5, 'If any of you lacks wisdom, let him ask God, who gives generously to all without reproach, and it will be given him.' Lord, I ask for your wisdom to guide my children's decisions, that they may walk in the path of righteousness. I thank you for filling their minds with discernment and understanding. In Jesus' name, amen.

Declaration of Spiritual Strength:

Mighty God, I declare your strength upon my children's spirits. Your Word tells us in Ephesians 6:10, 'Finally, be strong in the Lord and in the strength of his might.' I pray that you empower my children with spiritual fortitude, that they may stand firm against the schemes of the enemy. I thank you for filling them with your Holy Spirit and granting them victory over spiritual battles. In Jesus' name, amen.

Declaration of Provision:

Faithful Father, I declare your abundant provision over my children. Your Word assures us in Philippians 4:19, 'And my God will supply every need of yours according to his riches in glory in Christ Jesus.' Lord, I trust in your promise to meet all their needs, whether physical, emotional, or spiritual. I thank you for your provision that exceeds all expectations. In Jesus' name, amen.

Declaration of Purpose:
Heavenly Father, I declare your purpose over my children's lives. Your Word reminds us in Jeremiah 29:11, 'For I know the plans I have for you, declares the Lord, plans for welfare and not for evil, to give you a future and a hope.' I pray that you reveal and unfold your perfect plan for my children, guiding them into the destiny you have ordained for them. I thank you for using them mightily for your glory. In Jesus' name, amen.

Ask God to strengthen your children's faith:

One of the greatest gifts you can pray for your children is a strong and vibrant faith. Praying for their faith to grow involves asking God to deepen their understanding of His Word, to give them a hunger for His presence, and to strengthen their relationship with Him. The apostle John expressed his joy in knowing that his spiritual children were walking in the truth (3 John 1:4), highlighting the importance of praying for the growth and steadfastness of your children's faith.

Heavenly Father, I declare that you will strengthen my children's faith, empowering them to stand firm in the face of spiritual battles. I claim Isaiah 41:10 over their lives: "Fear not, for I am with you; be not dismayed, for I am your God; I will strengthen you, I will help you, I will uphold you with my righteous right hand."

Lord, I declare that you will establish a deep foundation of faith in my children's hearts, rooted in your Word. May they be like the wise man who built his house upon the rock, as stated in Matthew 7:24: "Everyone then who hears these words of mine and does them will be like a wise man who built his house on the rock."

Almighty God, I pray that you will equip my children with the full armor of God, as mentioned in Ephesians 6:11-13, so they can withstand the schemes of the enemy. Grant them the strength to "put on the whole armor of God, that [they] may be able to stand against the schemes of the devil."

Heavenly Father, I declare that you will surround my children with godly influences and mentors who will guide and encourage them in their faith journey. May they be inspired by the example of Paul's disciple, Timothy, as highlighted in 2 Timothy 1:5: "I am reminded of your sincere faith, a faith that dwelt first in your grandmother Lois and your mother Eunice and now, I am sure, dwells in you as well."

Lord, I declare that you will fill my children with Your Spirit, granting them wisdom, discernment, and a hunger for your truth. May they grow in their knowledge of you, as mentioned in Proverbs 2:6-7: "For the LORD gives wisdom; from his mouth come knowledge and understanding; he stores up sound wisdom for the upright; he is a shield to those who walk in integrity."

Pray for their protection from worldly influences:

In a world filled with distractions and temptations, it is essential to pray for your children's protection from the influence of the evil one. Jesus prayed for His disciples, asking the Father to keep them from the evil one (John 17:15). Similarly, you can intercede for your children, asking God to guard their hearts and minds, and to provide discernment and strength to resist worldly pressures.

Heavenly Father, I declare that my children are protected from the influence of the world, for your Word says in 1 John 2:15, "Do not love the world or anything in the world. If anyone loves the world, love for the Father is not in them." I pray that you would guard their hearts and minds, keeping them focused on you and your ways.

Lord, I declare that my children are covered by the armor of God, as stated in Ephesians 6:11, "Put on the full armor of God, so that you can take your stand against the devil's schemes." I pray that you would equip them with the belt of truth, the breastplate of righteousness, the shield of faith, the helmet of salvation, and the sword of the Spirit, so that they may resist the temptations and deceptions of the world.

Heavenly Father, I declare that my children walk in wisdom and discernment, as your Word teaches in Proverbs 2:11, "Discretion will protect you, and understanding will guard you." I pray that you would grant them discernment to recognize and avoid the snares and traps set by the enemy, and that they may make wise choices according to your will.

Lord, I declare that my children are set apart for your purposes, as declared in Romans 12:2, "Do not conform to the pattern of this world but be transformed by the renewing of your mind. Then you will be able to test and approve what God's will is—his good, pleasing and perfect will." I pray that you would mold their hearts and minds, transforming them into vessels that honor and serve you, rather than conforming to worldly values and influences.

Heavenly Father, I declare that my children are surrounded by your angels, as promised in Psalm 34:7, "The angel of the Lord encamps around those who fear him, and he delivers them." I pray that you would station your angels around them, protecting them from harm, guiding their steps, and preserving them from the negative influences of the world.

Pray for godly friendships and mentors for your children:

The company we keep greatly influences our lives. Praying for your children to have godly friendships and mentors involves asking God to bring positive influences into their lives. Proverbs 13:20 reminds us that those who walk with the wise become wise, while the companions of fools suffer harm. Seek God's guidance in leading your children to friends and mentors who will encourage their spiritual growth and character development.

Heavenly Father, I declare that you will guide my children to friends who will encourage their spiritual growth and character development. May they find companions who walk in your ways, seeking after righteousness and truth. Proverbs 13:20 says, "Walk with the wise and become wise, for a companion of fools suffers harm." Lead them to godly friendships that will shape their lives positively.

Lord, I pray that you will connect my children with mentors who will guide and inspire them in their spiritual journey. Raise up godly individuals who will pour wisdom, knowledge, and understanding into their lives. Proverbs 27:17 reminds us that "As iron sharpens iron, so one person sharpens another." Bring mentors into their lives who will challenge and encourage them to grow in their faith.

Gracious God, I declare that my children will be surrounded by friends who will speak words of life and encouragement. Protect them from negative influences and toxic relationships that can hinder their spiritual progress. Proverbs 18:24 assures us that "A man of many companions may come to ruin, but there is a friend who sticks closer than a brother." Lead them to friends who will stand by them and uplift them in their faith.

Heavenly Father, I pray that you will place my children in communities and groups where they can thrive spiritually. Lead them to churches, youth groups, and fellowship gatherings where they can grow alongside other believers. Hebrews 10:25 encourages us to "not giving up meeting together, as some are in the habit of doing, but encouraging one another." Provide them with a supportive spiritual community that will nurture their faith.

Lord, I declare that my children will be lights in their friendships and mentorship relationships, shining your love and truth. May their lives reflect your character and draw others closer to you. Matthew 5:16 reminds us, "In the same way, let your light shine before others, that they may see your good deeds and glorify your Father in heaven." Use my children to influence their friends and mentors positively, pointing them towards you.

Intercede for their physical health:

Good health is essential for your children's overall well-being. By praying for their physical health, you acknowledge that God is the ultimate healer and sustainer of life. Pray for their strength, vitality, and protection from illness. Remember the apostle John's prayer for his spiritual children in 3 John 1:2, where he expressed his desire for their physical well-being alongside their spiritual growth.

Heavenly Father, I declare divine protection and strength over my children's physical health. According to Psalm 91:11, I trust that you will command your angels to guard them in all their ways, shielding them from any harm or sickness.

Lord Jesus, I declare that my children's bodies are temples of the Holy Spirit, as stated in 1 Corinthians 6:19-20. I pray that you will empower them to make wise choices regarding their health and enable them to glorify you in their bodies.

Gracious God, I declare your promise of healing over my children's physical ailments. According to Jeremiah 30:17, I believe that you will restore their health and heal their wounds. I trust in your healing power to touch and mend every part of their bodies.

Almighty God, I declare victory over any genetic predispositions or hereditary conditions that may threaten my children's physical well-being. In Deuteronomy 7:15, you promised to keep your people free from all diseases. I claim this promise for my children and declare that they are free from any inherited ailments.

Heavenly Father, I declare supernatural vitality and energy over my children's physical bodies. In Isaiah 40:29, it says that you give power to the weak and strength to the weary. I ask you to renew their strength, granting them the energy and vigor to fulfill your purposes in their lives.

Pray for their emotional well-being:

Emotional well-being is crucial for your children's mental and psychological health. Praying for their emotional well-being involves asking God to grant them joy, peace, and stability. Romans 15:13 reminds us that God is the God of hope who can fill us with joy and peace as we trust in Him. Intercede for your children's emotional health, asking God to guide them through challenging circumstances and to grant them inner strength and resilience.

Plead for their academic and educational success:

Education plays a significant role in shaping your children's future. Praying for their academic success involves asking God to provide them with wisdom, knowledge, and understanding as they pursue their studies. Luke 2:52 describes how Jesus increased in wisdom and stature, indicating the importance of growth and development in various areas of life. Pray for your children's intellectual growth, that they may excel in their educational endeavors.

Ask God to protect their hearts from bitterness and unforgiveness:

The world can be a place where hurts and offenses can lead to bitterness and unforgiveness. Praying for your children to have hearts filled with forgiveness and compassion involves asking God to guard their hearts against bitterness and to help them extend forgiveness to others. Ephesians

4:31-32 urges us to put away bitterness and instead be kind, tenderhearted, and forgiving, just as God forgave us.

Pray for their purity and sexual integrity:

In a culture saturated with sexual imagery and immorality, it is vital to pray for your children's purity and sexual integrity. Praying for their purity involves asking God to protect their minds, hearts, and bodies from impurity and to instill in them a desire to honor Him with their actions. Psalm 119:9 teaches that keeping one's way pure involves guarding it according to God's Word. Seek God's help in guiding your children to make wise and righteous choices regarding their sexuality.

Pray for their relationships with siblings and family members:

Family relationships have a significant impact on a child's upbringing. Praying for your children's relationships with their siblings and family members involves asking God to cultivate love, harmony, and respect among them. Colossians 3:12-13 encourages us to be compassionate, kind, and forgiving, emphasizing the importance of nurturing healthy relationships within the family. Seek God's guidance in fostering an atmosphere of love and unity among your children.

Pray for their future spouses:

While it may seem early to pray for your children's future spouses, interceding for their future partners is an act of faith and trust in God's plan. Praying for their future spouses involves asking God to prepare and guide the person they will one day marry. Proverbs 18:22 highlights the importance of finding a godly spouse. Entrust your children's future marriages into God's hands, asking Him to bring the right person into their lives at the appointed time.

Ask for their protection against peer pressure:

Peer pressure can exert a strong influence on your children's choices and behavior. Praying for their protection against peer pressure involves asking God to strengthen them to resist negative influences and to empower them to stand firm in their convictions. Philippians 4:13 assures us that we can do all things through Christ who strengthens us. Pray that your children will find their identity in Christ and be confident in their values, enabling them to navigate peer pressure with wisdom and courage.

Pray for their spiritual growth and hunger for God's Word:

Spiritual growth is foundational for a thriving Christian life. Praying for your children's spiritual growth involves asking God to deepen their hunger for His Word, to open their hearts to receive His truth, and to empower them to live out their faith. 1 Peter 2:2 compares spiritual growth to newborn infants craving pure spiritual milk. Seek God's guidance in nurturing your children's spiritual development and providing opportunities for them to grow closer to Him.

Intercede for their career choices and vocational guidance:

As your children mature, they will face decisions about their careers and vocations. Praying for their career choices involves asking God to guide them, reveal their talents and passions, and direct them to paths that align with His purposes for their lives. Proverbs 16:3 encourages us to commit our work to the Lord and trust that He will establish our plans. Seek God's wisdom and counsel as you pray for your children's future careers.

Pray for their financial stewardship:

Financial wisdom and responsible stewardship are essential life skills. Praying for your children's financial well-being involves asking God to teach them principles of wise money management, to provide for their needs, and to bless their financial endeavors. Philippians 4:19 assures us that God will supply all our needs according to His riches in glory. Teach your children the importance of seeking God's guidance in their finances and trusting in His provision.

Ask God to protect them from addiction and harmful habits:

The world is filled with various addictions and harmful habits that can ensnare your children. Praying for their protection involves asking God to shield them from addictive behaviors and to grant them strength and self-control. Galatians 5:1 reminds us that Christ has set us free for true freedom, and we can resist the yoke of slavery. Pray that your children will find their fulfillment and satisfaction in God alone, avoiding the snares of addiction.

Pray for their leadership skills and influence:

Each child has the potential to positively impact others and make a difference in the world. Praying for their leadership skills involves asking God to develop their character, wisdom, and servant-heartedness, preparing them to lead with integrity and compassion. Mark 10:43 teaches that true greatness is found in being a servant. Pray that your children will be servant leaders, using their influence to inspire and uplift others.

Plead for their resilience in the face of challenges:

Life is full of challenges, and it is crucial to pray for your children's resilience and perseverance. Pleading for their resilience involves asking God to strengthen them during difficult times, to give them courage to face adversity, and to use challenges as opportunities for growth. 2 Corinthians 12:9 reminds us that God's power is made perfect in weakness. Pray that your children will lean on God's strength and experience His grace as they navigate life's ups and downs.

Pray for their compassion and empathy towards others:

Cultivating a heart of compassion and empathy is vital for your children's character development. Praying for their compassion involves asking God to fill their hearts with kindness, humility, and a genuine concern for others. Colossians 3:12 encourages us to be compassionate and forgiving, just as God has forgiven us. Intercede for your children's hearts, that they may be vessels of love and compassion in a world that desperately needs it.

Ask for protection from spiritual attacks and temptations:

Spiritual warfare is a reality, and it is essential to pray for your children's protection from spiritual attacks and temptations. Asking for protection involves seeking God's shield against the schemes of the enemy, and His guidance in making wise and righteous choices. James 4:7 teaches us to submit to God, resist the devil, and watch him flee. Pray for your children's spiritual armor and discernment, that they may stand firm against the enemy's tactics.

Finally, thank God for hearing and answering your prayers:

Prayer is a powerful tool, and as you fight for your children on your knees, remember to express gratitude to God for hearing and answering your prayers. Philippians 4:6 encourages us not to be anxious but to present our requests to God with thanksgiving. Trust that God is faithful and that He is working in the lives of your children, even when you may not see immediate results. Thank Him for His love, grace, and the privilege of partnering with Him through prayer.

"Pray in the language of heaven (Pray in tongues) for at least 10 minutes as you enter into the court of heaven to plead you case; if you cannot pray in tongues, enter His court with praise and worship for at least 10 minutes before you plead your case."

Warfare Prayers:

1. I declare that my children are protected by the mighty hand of God. (Psalm 91:11)
2. I declare that no weapon formed against my children shall prosper. (Isaiah 54:17)
3. I declare that my children walk in the favor and blessings of the Lord. (Psalm 5:12)
4. I declare that God's angels encamp around my children, guarding them in all their ways. (Psalm 34:7)
5. I declare that my children are filled with the wisdom and discernment of the Holy Spirit. (James 1:5)
6. I declare that my children are rooted and grounded in God's love, fearlessly standing against evil. (Ephesians 3:17)
7. I declare that my children have a sound mind, free from anxiety and fear. (2 Timothy 1:7)

8. I declare that my children are overcomers in Christ, victorious in every battle they face. (1 John 5:4)
9. I declare that my children are protected from sickness and disease. (Psalm 91:10)
10. I declare that my children walk in integrity and righteousness before God and men. (Proverbs 20:7)
11. I declare that my children are surrounded by godly influences and wise mentors. (Proverbs 13:20)
12. I declare that my children have a hunger and thirst for God's Word, growing in spiritual maturity. (1 Peter 2:2)
13. I declare that my children are covered by the blood of Jesus, washed clean from sin. (1 John 1:7)
14. I declare that my children are led by the Holy Spirit, making wise decisions in every area of their lives. (Galatians 5:25)
15. I declare that my children have a heart of gratitude, always giving thanks to God. (Colossians 3:17)
16. I declare that my children have a spirit of excellence, excelling in their studies and pursuits. (Daniel 6:3)
17. I declare that my children have courage and boldness to stand for their faith. (Joshua 1:9)
18. I declare that my children are protected from the snares and traps of the enemy. (Psalm 141:9)
19. I declare that my children are filled with joy and peace that surpasses all understanding. (Romans 15:13)
20. I declare that my children have a heart of compassion and love for others. (1 John 4:7)

21. I declare that my children have a spirit of forgiveness, releasing any bitterness or resentment. (Ephesians 4:32)
22. I declare that my children have the strength and courage to resist peer pressure and make godly choices. (1 Corinthians 16:13)
23. I declare that my children have divine health and walk in wholeness. (3 John 1:2)
24. I declare that my children are protected from any harm or danger that may come their way. (Psalm 121:7)
25. I declare that my children have a heart that seeks after God, desiring His presence above all else. (Psalm 27:8)
26. I declare that my children are set apart for God's purposes and walk in their calling. (Jeremiah 1:5)
27. I declare that my children are surrounded by godly friendships that sharpen and encourage them. (Proverbs 27:17)
28. I declare that my children have the peace of God that guards their hearts and minds. (Philippians 4:7)
29. I declare that my children have a spirit of humility, serving others with love. (Philippians 2:3)
30. I declare that my children have supernatural protection in their travels and journeys. (Psalm 121:8)
31. I declare that my children have a heart of obedience, honoring authority and following God's commands. (Exodus 20:12)
32. I declare that my children have discernment to recognize and avoid deception and falsehood. (1 John 4:1)
33. I declare that my children have a hunger for righteousness, seeking first the kingdom of God. (Matthew 6:33)

34. I declare that my children are covered by the blood of Jesus, breaking every generational curse. (Galatians 3:13)
35. I declare that my children have a spirit of perseverance, enduring in faith through trials. (James 1:12)
36. I declare that my children have a heart of gratitude, acknowledging God's goodness in their lives. (Psalm 100:4)
37. I declare that my children have divine wisdom to make right choices in relationships. (Proverbs 13:20)
38. I declare that my children have a heart of worship, glorifying God with their lives. (Psalm 95:6)
39. I declare that my children have a spirit of humility, esteeming others above themselves. (Philippians 2:4)
40. I declare that my children have supernatural provision for all their needs. (Philippians 4:19)
41. I declare that my children have a spirit of unity and love, building strong relationships with their siblings. (Psalm 133:1)
42. I declare that my children have a passion for evangelism, sharing the gospel with boldness. (Matthew 28:19-20)
43. I declare that my children have a heart of forgiveness, extending grace to others. (Colossians 3:13)
44. I declare that my children have a spirit of contentment, finding joy in every circumstance. (Philippians 4:11)
45. I declare that my children have a spirit of purity, guarding their hearts and minds. (Psalm 119:9)
46. I declare that my children have a spirit of generosity, giving freely to those in need. (2 Corinthians 9:7)

47. I declare that my children have divine protection from any accidents or harm. (Psalm 91:4)
48. I declare that my children have a heart that seeks after God, hungering for His presence. (Psalm 27:4)
49. I declare that my children have supernatural favor in their education and learning. (Luke 2:52)
50. I declare that my children have a spirit of thanksgiving, expressing gratitude to God in all things. (1 Thessalonians 5:18)

Chapter 11

The Mother's Mandate: Empowering Warrior Moms to Stand in the Court of Heaven

Warrior Moms, also known as mothers who fervently pray and intercede for their children, play a crucial role in shaping the spiritual well-being of their families. These courageous women engage in spiritual warfare, seeking God's guidance, protection, and blessings for their loved ones. To empower Warrior Moms to stand confidently in the Court of Heaven, it is essential to understand their biblical foundation and equip them with the necessary tools. Let's explore key principles from the Bible that empower Warrior Moms to boldly approach the Court of Heaven on behalf of their children.

The Power of Prayer:

The Bible encourages believers to pray without ceasing (1 Thessalonians 5:17). Warrior Moms understand the significance of fervent and persistent prayer. They recognize that their intercession can influence the spiritual realm and bring about God's intervention in the lives of their children. By seeking God's face in prayer, they tap into the divine power that can change circumstances and shape destinies.

Prayer Declaration for a Strong Spiritual Foundation:

Heavenly Father, I thank you for the privilege of being a Warrior Mom. I declare that my children will grow up with a strong spiritual foundation. I pray that they will have a deep and personal relationship with you. I intercede for their hearts to be receptive to your Word, and that they will walk in your truth all the days of their lives. May your Spirit guide them and protect them from the snares of the enemy. In Jesus' name, amen.

Prayer Declaration for Divine Guidance:

Dear Lord, I lift up my children before you in prayer. I declare that they will walk in your perfect will and purpose for their lives. I pray that you will guide their steps and direct their paths. May your wisdom and discernment be upon them as they navigate through life's challenges. I declare that they will make wise choices and follow the path of righteousness. In the name of Jesus, I claim your divine guidance and leading over their lives. Amen.

Prayer Declaration for Protection from Harm:

Mighty God, I stand in the Court of Heaven on behalf of my children. I declare your promise of protection over them. I plead the blood of Jesus as a covering over their lives, shielding them from all harm and danger. I rebuke every plan of the enemy to bring harm to their bodies, minds, or spirits. I trust in your unfailing love and faithfulness to watch over them day and night. Thank you, Lord, for being their ultimate Protector. In Jesus' name, I pray, amen.

Prayer Declaration for Spiritual Discernment:

Gracious Father, I pray for my children's spiritual discernment. I declare that they will have a deep understanding of your Word and the ability to discern truth from falsehood. I pray that you will sharpen their spiritual senses to recognize the schemes and lies of the enemy. Fill them with your Spirit of discernment, enabling them to make godly choices and avoid deception. I declare that they will be guided by your truth and walk in spiritual discernment all the days of their lives. In Jesus' name, I declare this, amen.

Prayer Declaration for Divine Favor:

Heavenly Father, I come before you as a Warrior Mom, seeking your divine favor upon my children. I declare that they will find favor with you and with others. May doors of opportunity open before them, and may they walk in the favor that brings success and blessings. I pray that you will surround them with godly mentors and influencers who will help them grow in their faith and purpose. I trust in your abundant grace and favor to be poured out upon their lives. In Jesus' name, I declare your favor over my children, amen.

The Authority of Believers:

In the Court of Heaven, Warrior Moms can stand with confidence, knowing they have been given authority through Jesus Christ. Jesus said, "Behold, I have given you authority to tread on serpents and scorpions, and over all the power of the enemy" (Luke 10:19). Empowered by this authority, Warrior Moms can boldly approach the Court of Heaven, speaking forth God's promises and declaring victory over the forces of darkness that may seek to harm their children.

Declaration of Authority:
In the name of Jesus, I declare my authority as a believer over the enemy. I stand firm in the power bestowed upon me by Christ and confidently command every force of darkness to flee from my children's lives. No weapon formed against them shall prosper, for I have been given authority to overcome all the power of the enemy.

Declaration of Protection:
Heavenly Father, I thank you for the authority you have given me. I declare that my children are covered by the precious blood of Jesus. I rebuke every plan, scheme, and attack of the enemy against them. I release the angelic hosts to encamp around them, guarding and protecting them from all harm.

Declaration of Victory:
I proclaim victory over the enemy in the lives of my children. Satan, you have no power or authority over them. By the authority of Jesus, I dismantle every stronghold, break every chain, and release them from every bondage. I declare that my children walk in freedom, joy, and the abundant life that Christ has promised.

Declaration of God's Word:

I declare the Word of God as a sword against the enemy's lies and deception. I speak forth Scriptures of truth, declaring that my children are more than conquerors through Christ who strengthens them. I declare that they are blessed, favored, and destined for greatness according to God's perfect plan for their lives.

Declaration of Peace and Blessing:
I declare peace and blessings over my children's lives. I speak shalom, the peace of God, that surpasses all understanding, to guard their hearts and minds in Christ Jesus. I declare that they walk in divine health, prosperity, and the fullness of God's goodness. I release God's favor upon them, opening doors of opportunity and success in every area of their lives.

The Promise of Protection:

God's Word assures Warrior Moms of His unwavering protection over their children. Proverbs 22:6 states, "Train up a child in the way he should go; even when he is old, he will not depart from it." By diligently teaching their children God's ways, Warrior Moms sow seeds of righteousness and invite divine protection. They can approach the Court of Heaven, appealing to God's promise to safeguard their children from the enemy's schemes.

Heavenly Father, I thank You for Your promise of protection over my children. I declare that as I train them in Your ways, they will not depart from it. I entrust them into Your loving care, knowing that You will shield them from the schemes of the enemy. May Your divine protection be a constant presence in their lives, guarding them against harm and leading them on the path of righteousness.

Lord, I declare Your promise from Psalm 91:11-12, that You will command Your angels concerning my children, to guard them in all their ways. I pray for a hedge of angelic protection around them, that no weapon formed against them shall prosper. I trust in Your faithfulness to shield them from dangers seen and unseen, and I thank You for watching over them with vigilant eyes.

Heavenly Father, Your Word assures me that You are a refuge and fortress for my children in times of trouble (Psalm 46:1). I declare that they dwell in the secret place of the Most High, abiding under the shadow of Your wings. I pray that they will find safety, comfort, and strength in Your presence, knowing that nothing can separate them from Your love and protection.

Lord, I declare Your promise from Isaiah 54:17 that no weapon formed against my children shall prosper. I stand in the Court of Heaven, decreeing that every plan, scheme, or attack of the enemy aimed at my children's well-being and destiny is nullified and rendered powerless. I thank You for being their defender and for granting them victory in every battle they face.

Heavenly Father, I declare Your promise from Proverbs 18:10 that the name of the Lord is a strong tower, and my children can run to it and find safety. I pray that they will always seek refuge in You, finding strength and peace in Your presence. I thank You for surrounding them with Your divine protection, shielding them from the snares of the enemy, and preserving their lives for Your purposes.

The Weapon of Scripture:

Scripture is a powerful weapon that Warrior Moms can employ in their spiritual battles. Hebrews 4:12 declares, "For the word of God is living and active, sharper than any two-edged sword." By meditating on and declaring God's Word, Warrior Moms can overcome the lies and deceptions of the enemy. Armed with the truth, they can effectively plead their case in the Court of Heaven, aligning their prayers with God's promises.

Declaration of Victory:
Heavenly Father, I declare that your Word is a powerful weapon in my hands. I affirm that as I meditate on and declare your promises, I walk in victory over every scheme of the enemy. Your Word is living and active, and it brings forth transformation and breakthrough in the lives of my children. I thank you for the authority I have through Christ, and I declare that every plan of the enemy is rendered powerless by the truth of your Word. In Jesus' name, I claim victory for my children and their spiritual well-being.

Declaration of Protection:

Gracious God, I thank you for the promise of protection found in your Word. I declare that as I teach and train my children in your ways, they are shielded from the attacks of the enemy. Your Word says, "No weapon formed against them shall prosper" (Isaiah 54:17). I boldly declare this truth over my children, affirming that they are hidden in your loving embrace. I pray that you would surround them with your angels and keep them safe from every harm and danger. In the name of Jesus, I release your divine protection over my children.

Declaration of Wisdom and Guidance:

Heavenly Father, I acknowledge that your Word is a lamp unto my feet and a light unto my path (Psalm 119:105). I declare that as I seek wisdom and guidance for my children, your Word will be my guide. I pray that you would illuminate their paths and lead them in your perfect will. I declare that they have the mind of Christ and that the Holy Spirit dwells within them, guiding their decisions and choices. I trust in your faithfulness to direct their steps and shape their destinies according to your purposes. In Jesus' name, I declare wisdom and guidance over my children.

Declaration of Identity and Purpose:

Loving Father, I declare that your Word reveals the true identity and purpose of my children. I affirm that they are fearfully and wonderfully made (Psalm 139:14), created for a specific plan and calling. I reject every lie and negative influence that seeks to distort their sense of self-worth. I declare that they are chosen, loved, and called by you. I pray that they would walk in the confidence of their identity as sons and daughters of the Most High God. May they fulfill the purpose you have ordained for their lives and bring glory to your name. In the powerful name of Jesus, I declare identity and purpose over my children.

Declaration of Spiritual Growth:
Gracious God, I declare that your Word is a seed that takes root in the hearts of my children. I pray that as they encounter your truth, it would produce spiritual growth and maturity within them. I declare that they will hunger and thirst for your Word, delighting in its teachings. I pray that you would open their eyes to understand your truth and empower them to apply it to their lives. I declare that they will grow in faith, wisdom, and knowledge of you. May their lives be a testimony of your transforming power. In Jesus' name, I declare spiritual growth over my children.

The Support of the Church:

Warrior Moms should not walk this journey alone but seek the support and encouragement of fellow believers. Hebrews 10:24-25 encourages believers to "consider how to stir up one another to love and good works, not neglecting to meet together." Through the fellowship of the church, Warrior Moms can find strength, accountability, and collective intercession. Together, they can stand in unity, petitioning the Court of Heaven on behalf of their families.

Heavenly Father, I declare that you have placed me in a supportive church community that understands the power of intercession. Thank you for surrounding me with fellow believers who are committed to stirring up love and good works in my life and the lives of my children.

Lord, I pray for unity and strength within my church family. May we be bound together by the love of Christ, supporting and encouraging one another as we navigate the challenges of parenting. Help us to be a source of comfort, wisdom, and accountability for each other.

Father, I declare that my church is a place where the Word of God is faithfully preached and taught. Grant our pastors and leaders divine wisdom and revelation as they guide us in the ways of righteousness. May the preaching of your Word equip and empower us to fulfill our roles as Warrior Moms.

Lord, I lift up the intercessory prayer ministries in my church. I pray that they will be strengthened and grow in number. Raise up mighty prayer warriors who will stand in the gap for families, lifting up our concerns and seeking your divine intervention on behalf of our children.

Heavenly Father, I declare that my church is a safe haven where I can openly share my burdens, joys, and struggles as a Warrior Mom. I thank you for the caring hearts and listening ears that are ready to support and pray with me. May my church family be a source of comfort and encouragement, reminding me that I am not alone in my journey.

Warrior Moms are an invaluable force in the spiritual lives of their children and families. By understanding their biblical foundation and utilizing the tools provided by God, they can be empowered to stand confidently in the Court of Heaven. Through fervent prayer, the authority of believers, the promise of protection, the weapon of Scripture, and the support of the church, Warrior Moms can approach the throne of grace with boldness, seeking God's guidance, intervention, and blessings for their loved ones. May every Warrior Mom be equipped and empowered to fulfill their vital role as intercessors and spiritual warriors in the lives of their children.

> ***"Pray in the language of heaven (Pray in tongues) for at least 10 minutes as you enter into the court of heaven to plead you case; if you cannot pray in tongues, enter His court with praise and worship for at least 10 minutes before you plead your case."***

Warfare Prayers:

1. I declare that I am clothed in the full armor of God: the belt of truth, the breastplate of righteousness, the readiness of the gospel of peace on my feet, the shield of faith, the helmet of salvation, and the sword of the Spirit (Ephesians 6:13-17).
2. I proclaim that I am more than a conqueror through Christ who loves me (Romans 8:37).

3. I renounce any spirit of fear and declare that God has not given me a spirit of fear, but of power, love, and a sound mind (2 Timothy 1:7).
4. I decree that no weapon formed against me shall prosper, and every tongue that rises against me in judgment, I shall condemn (Isaiah 54:17).
5. I declare that the Lord is my strength and my shield; my heart trusts in Him, and I am helped (Psalm 28:7).
6. I plead the blood of Jesus over my life, covering and protecting me from all evil (Revelation 12:11).
7. I command every assignment of the enemy against me to be exposed and rendered ineffective in the name of Jesus (Ephesians 5:11).
8. I declare that I am seated with Christ in heavenly places, far above all principalities and powers (Ephesians 2:6).
9. I bind and rebuke every demonic force that seeks to hinder my progress and destiny in Christ (Matthew 18:18).
10. I declare that the Lord goes before me, making every crooked path straight and every rough place smooth (Isaiah 45:2).
11. I proclaim that I am a child of God, and the evil one cannot touch me (1 John 5:18).
12. I declare that the angel of the Lord encamps around me and delivers me from all harm (Psalm 34:7).
13. I break and cancel every generational curse that may be operating in my life, in the name of Jesus (Galatians 3:13).

14. I declare that I am rooted and grounded in the love of Christ, and nothing can separate me from His love (Ephesians 3:17-19).
15. I renounce and cast out every spirit of heaviness, depression, and anxiety, replacing them with the garment of praise (Isaiah 61:3).
16. I declare that I am more than a conqueror in all things through Christ who strengthens me (Romans 8:37).
17. I command every demonic stronghold in my life to be demolished by the power of the Holy Spirit (2 Corinthians 10:4-5).
18. I proclaim that I am the righteousness of God in Christ Jesus, and my prayers avail much (James 5:16).
19. I rebuke and cast out every spirit of infirmity and declare divine health and wholeness over my body (Luke 10:19).
20. I declare that no weapon formed against my mind shall prosper, and I have the mind of Christ (1 Corinthians 2:16).
21. I bind and cast out every spirit of confusion and declare clarity and wisdom to guide my steps (James 1:5).
22. I decree that I walk in divine favor, and God's goodness and mercy follow me all the days of my life (Psalm 23:6).
23. I declare that I am a vessel of honor, sanctified and useful for the Master's work (2 Timothy 2:21).
24. I break and cancel every word curse spoken against me, replacing them with blessings and favor (Proverbs 18:21).
25. I declare that I am the head and not the tail, above and not beneath, in every area of my life (Deuteronomy 28:13).
26. I proclaim that God has not given me a spirit of timidity, but of power, love, and self-discipline (2 Timothy 1:7).

27. I renounce and cast out every spirit of strife and division, replacing it with the spirit of unity and peace (Ephesians 4:3).
28. I declare that I am a temple of the Holy Spirit, and no defiling spirit can dwell within me (1 Corinthians 6:19).
29. I rebuke and cast out every spirit of failure and declare success and prosperity in my endeavors (Joshua 1:8).
30. I declare that I am the salt of the earth and the light of the world, shining brightly for the glory of God (Matthew 5:13-14).
31. I break and nullify every evil decree or enchantment spoken against me, by the power in the name of Jesus (Numbers 23:23).
32. I proclaim that I have authority over serpents and scorpions, and nothing shall by any means harm me (Luke 10:19).
33. I declare that the plans of the enemy shall not prevail in my life, for God's purpose and destiny will be fulfilled (Isaiah 46:10-11).
34. I renounce and cast out every spirit of discouragement and declare divine encouragement and strength in my spirit (Psalm 138:3).
35. I bind and cast out every spirit of procrastination, laziness, and complacency, and I embrace a spirit of diligence and excellence (Proverbs 12:24).
36. I declare that the peace of God, which surpasses all understanding, guards my heart and mind in Christ Jesus (Philippians 4:7).
37. I rebuke and cast out every spirit of witchcraft and declare that no weapon formed against me shall prosper (Isaiah 54:17).
38. I declare that I am anointed and empowered by the Holy Spirit to fulfill my God-given purpose (Acts 1:8).

39. I break and cancel every word curse spoken over my life, and I release blessings and favor in their place (Proverbs 26:2).
40. I declare that God has given His angels charge over me to guard me in all my ways (Psalm 91:11).
41. I renounce and cast out every spirit of doubt and unbelief, embracing a faith that moves mountains (Mark 11:22-24).
42. I declare that I am more than a conqueror through Him who loved me, and nothing can separate me from His love (Romans 8:38-39).
43. I command every door of opportunity that the enemy has closed to be opened by the hand of God (Revelation 3:8).
44. I proclaim that the joy of the Lord is my strength, and I walk in the abundance of His joy (Nehemiah 8:10).
45. I renounce and cast out every spirit of poverty and lack, declaring that God supplies all my needs according to His riches in glory (Philippians 4:19).
46. I declare that I am a chosen generation, a royal priesthood, and a holy nation, called out of darkness into God's marvelous light (1 Peter 2:9).
47. I break and cancel every soul tie and ungodly attachment that may hinder my spiritual growth and freedom (1 Corinthians 6:17).
48. I declare that I am a woman of faith, and I walk by faith and not by sight (2 Corinthians 5:7).
49. I renounce and cast out every spirit of stagnation and declare divine acceleration and progress in every area of my life (Isaiah 40:31).

50. I declare that I am victorious in Christ Jesus, and I overcome by the blood of the Lamb and the word of my testimony (Revelation 12:11).

Chapter 12

Warrior Mom's Battle Against the Spirit of the Street: Protecting Her Children with Biblical Principles

In today's world, parenting has become a challenging endeavor, as children are increasingly exposed to various negative influences, including the spirit of the street. This term refers to the negative influences and temptations that prevail in urban environments, often leading children astray. However, amidst these challenges, there are warrior moms who, empowered by their faith and armed with the Word of God, fight against these negative influences to protect their children.

Understanding the Spirit of the Street:

The spirit of the street represents a collection of negative influences such as drugs, violence, peer pressure, and moral degradation that children often encounter in urban environments. These influences can have a detrimental impact on the well-being and spiritual development of young minds. A warrior mom recognizes the dangers posed by this spirit and endeavors to shield her children from its grasp.

Heavenly Father, I come before you with a humble heart, seeking wisdom and understanding concerning the spirit of the street that threatens my children. Grant me discernment to recognize the negative influences that surround them, and the strength to shield them from harm.

Lord, open the eyes of my children to see the dangers and temptations that arise from the spirit of the street. Give them a spirit of discernment to distinguish right from wrong, and the courage to resist peer pressure and negative influences.

Father, I pray for a spirit of wisdom and understanding to guide me in effectively communicating with my children about the spirit of the street. Help me to convey the seriousness of these influences while nurturing their hearts with love, compassion, and understanding.

Lord, I declare your divine protection over my children as they navigate the challenges of the street. Surround them with your angels, placing a hedge of safety around them, and guard their hearts and minds from the allure of negative influences.

Heavenly Father, equip me with the tools and knowledge I need to combat the spirit of the street. Grant me insight into their world so that I may effectively guide my children, instilling in them biblical principles and godly values that will serve as their shield against the darkness that surrounds them. In Jesus' name. Amen.

The Role of a Warrior Mom:

A warrior mom takes on the responsibility of guiding and protecting her children, instilling in them godly values and principles that act as a shield against the spirit of the street. By being actively involved in their lives, she creates a nurturing environment that helps her children grow spiritually and resist negative influences. The Bible provides numerous references that offer guidance and inspiration to warrior moms in their battle.

Declaration of Protection:
Heavenly Father, I declare your divine protection over my children. Surround them with your angels and shield them from the negative influences of the spirit of the street. May your presence be a fortress around them, guarding their hearts and minds from harm.

Declaration of Wisdom:
Lord, I pray for wisdom and discernment as I guide my children in the ways of righteousness. Grant me the insight to teach them your commandments and the teachings of Jesus, so that they may walk in your truth and resist the temptations of the world.

Declaration of Strength:
God, I declare strength and resilience for myself as a warrior mom. When I face challenges and discouragement, empower me with your Holy Spirit to stand firm in my commitment to raise godly children. Fill me with courage and determination to overcome any obstacles that come our way.

Declaration of Guidance:

Gracious Father, I humbly seek your guidance in every decision I make for my children. Direct my steps and help me lead by example, reflecting your love, forgiveness, and compassion. Guide me in establishing boundaries and disciplining my children with love, so that they may grow in wisdom and righteousness.

Declaration of Faith:
Lord, I declare unwavering faith in your promises and your faithfulness. I trust that as I commit my children into your hands, you will watch over them and fulfill your purpose in their lives. Strengthen my faith as I pray, knowing that you are always with us, fighting alongside me as the ultimate warrior.

Equipping Children with Biblical Truths:

A warrior mom understands the power of God's Word in shaping the hearts and minds of her children. She takes the time to teach them biblical truths, such as the Ten Commandments (Exodus 20:1-17) and the teachings of Jesus (Matthew 5-7), which promote righteousness, love, and compassion. These teachings act as a moral compass, helping children discern right from wrong when confronted with temptations from the spirit of the street.

Heavenly Father, I declare that your Word will be the foundation of my children's lives. I pray that you would open their hearts and minds to receive and understand your teachings. May they embrace the truth found in your Word and let it guide their thoughts, decisions, and actions.

Lord, I declare that my children will have a hunger and thirst for righteousness. I pray that they will develop a deep love for your Word, desiring to study it diligently and meditate on it day and night. May your Word become a lamp to their feet and a light to their path, leading them in the ways of righteousness.

Gracious God, I declare that you will empower my children with discernment and wisdom. In a world filled with conflicting messages and false teachings, I pray that they will have the ability to distinguish between truth and deception. May your Spirit guide them in all understanding, enabling them to make godly choices and avoid the snares of the enemy.

Lord, I declare that my children will be rooted and grounded in the love of Christ. I pray that they will grasp the depth of your love for them and understand the sacrifice Jesus made on the cross. May this knowledge strengthen their faith, anchor their identities in Christ, and empower them to share your love with others.

Heavenly Father, I declare that your Word will be a shield and a fortress around my children. I pray that it will protect them from the temptations and pressures of the spirit of the street. May your truth guard their hearts and minds, enabling them to stand firm in their faith, and embolden them to be a light in a dark world. In Jesus' name, I declare these prayers over my children, trusting in Your faithfulness to fulfill them. Amen.

Praying for Protection and Guidance:

Prayer is a vital weapon in the arsenal of a warrior mom. She fervently seeks God's protection and guidance for her children, knowing that He is the ultimate source of strength and wisdom. She prays for their safety, discernment, and strength to resist peer pressure and negative influences. The Bible reassures warrior moms of God's faithfulness and promises, providing solace and encouragement in their battle (Psalm 34:17-20, Isaiah 41:10).

Heavenly Father, I declare your divine protection over my children. I ask that you surround them with your angels, guarding them from the influences of the spirit of the street. Shield them from harm and keep them safe in your loving embrace.

Lord, I declare that you are their guide and counselor. I pray that you would grant them discernment and wisdom to navigate the challenges they face each day. Lead them on the path of righteousness and steer them away from the pitfalls of temptation.

Father, I declare that your word is a lamp unto their feet and a light unto their path. I pray that your truth would illuminate their minds and hearts, helping them make decisions that align with your will. May they find comfort and direction in the pages of Scripture.

Heavenly Father, I declare that you are their refuge and strength. In moments of weakness or vulnerability, I pray that they would find solace in your presence. Empower them to resist peer pressure and negative influences, knowing that you are their source of strength.

Lord, I declare that you are faithful to your promises. I trust in your faithfulness to watch over my children and guide them throughout their lives. I release any anxieties and fears into your hands and choose to rest in the assurance that you are working all things for their good.

Leading by Example:

Warrior moms understand that their own actions speak louder than words. They strive to exemplify godly character and integrity, demonstrating to their children how to live a life pleasing to God. By practicing forgiveness, humility, and kindness, they set a powerful example that helps their children navigate the challenges posed by the spirit of the street (Ephesians 5:1-2, Colossians 3:12-14).

Heavenly Father, I declare that I will walk in integrity and righteousness before my children, being a living example of your love and grace. Help me to demonstrate forgiveness, humility, and kindness in all my actions, so that my children may learn to emulate these virtues.

Lord, I declare that I will prioritize spending time in your presence, seeking your wisdom and guidance. By prioritizing my relationship with you, I will show my children the importance of seeking you first in all things and relying on your strength to overcome challenges.

Gracious God, I declare that I will be intentional in my words and actions, ensuring that they align with your Word. Let my speech be filled with words of encouragement, truth, and compassion, building up my children and pointing them towards your truth.

Heavenly Father, I declare that I will practice forgiveness and reconciliation in my relationships, modeling the power of reconciliation and restoration. Teach me to be quick to forgive, just as you have forgiven me, so that my children may witness the healing and transformation that comes from extending grace.

Lord, I declare that I will exhibit a servant's heart, willingly putting the needs of others before my own. Help me to serve my family with joy and selflessness, demonstrating the sacrificial love that you have shown us through Jesus Christ. May my children see the joy that comes from serving others and be inspired to do the same. In Jesus' name, I pray. Amen.

Establishing Boundaries and Disciplining with Love:

To protect their children from the spirit of the street, warrior moms set clear boundaries and guidelines based on biblical principles. They understand the importance of discipline as a means of correction and instruction. However, discipline is administered with love, ensuring that children understand the reasons behind it and learn from their mistakes. This approach fosters a sense of security and stability, reducing the allure of negative influences (Proverbs 22:6, Ephesians 6:4).

Heavenly Father, I declare that I will establish clear and godly boundaries for my children, guiding them in the path of righteousness. May these boundaries be rooted in your Word and principles, leading them away from the spirit of the street and towards a life of purpose and fulfillment.

Lord, I declare that as I discipline my children, I will do so with love and understanding. Help me to correct them gently, teaching them valuable lessons and instilling in them a sense of responsibility and self-discipline. May my discipline reflect your grace and mercy, guiding them towards a life of obedience and character.

Gracious God, I declare that I will seek wisdom and discernment as I discipline my children. Grant me the insight to know when discipline is necessary and the courage to follow through. Help me to discipline them not out of anger or frustration but with a heart filled with love, knowing that discipline is essential for their growth and development.

Heavenly Father, I declare that as I establish boundaries for my children, I will communicate with clarity and compassion. Grant me the words to explain the reasons behind the boundaries, helping them understand the importance of making godly choices. May our conversations be filled with love and understanding, fostering a bond of trust and respect between us.

Lord, I declare that I will discipline my children in a way that points them towards you. May my actions and words reflect your character, displaying patience, kindness, and forgiveness. Help me to discipline them not to crush their spirits but to mold them into the image of Christ, enabling them to walk in your ways and resist the temptations of the world. In Jesus' name, I pray. Amen.

Building a Supportive Community:

Warrior moms recognize the value of a supportive community in their battle against the spirit of the street. They seek out like-minded individuals who share their faith and commitment to raising godly children. By fostering connections with other parents, church communities, and mentors, warrior moms create a network of support that strengthens their resolve and provides additional resources for their children's spiritual growth (Proverbs 27:17, Hebrews 10:24-25).

Heavenly Father, I declare that you are the author of community, and I thank you for the divine connections you bring into my life. I pray for discernment to identify individuals who share my faith and commitment to raising godly children. May we come together to build a supportive community that uplifts and strengthens us on this journey.

Lord, I pray for genuine friendships and mentorship opportunities for myself and my children within our community. Surround us with people who will encourage and guide us, helping us grow in wisdom and understanding. Grant us divine connections that will inspire us to walk in your ways and stand strong against the spirit of the street.

Gracious God, I declare unity and harmony within our community. May we be bound together by a common purpose and a shared commitment to raise children who honor you. Help us to celebrate one another's victories, support each other in times of struggle, and always extend grace and love.

Heavenly Father, I lift up the leaders and mentors in our community. Grant them wisdom, discernment, and a heart filled with compassion as they guide and nurture our children. Strengthen their faith and empower them to be positive role models, imparting godly values and principles that will equip our children to withstand the challenges of the world.

Lord, I pray for divine opportunities to serve and bless others within our community. Help me to be a source of encouragement, offering a listening ear, a helping hand, and words of wisdom when needed. May our community be characterized by selflessness, kindness, and a genuine desire to uplift one another. In Jesus' name, I pray. Amen.

The battle against the spirit of the street is an ongoing challenge for parents, but warrior moms rise to the occasion, fortified by their faith and armed with the Word of God. By equipping their children with biblical truths, praying for protection, leading by example, establishing boundaries, and building a supportive community, they stand as guardians, shielding their children from the negative influences that pervade society. In the face of adversity, warrior moms exemplify strength, resilience, and unwavering faith, ensuring that their children grow up to be godly individuals who make a positive impact on the world around them.

"Pray in the language of heaven (Pray in tongues) for at least 10 minutes as you enter into the court of heaven to plead you case; if you cannot pray in tongues, enter His court with praise and worship for at least 10 minutes before you plead your case."

Warfare Prayers:

1. Heavenly Father, I declare that my children are protected by the blood of Jesus from any harm or danger on the streets. (Exodus 12:13)
2. I bind and rebuke every spirit of violence and crime that seeks to target my children, in the name of Jesus. (Luke 10:19)
3. I decree that my children walk in the light of righteousness, and no darkness can prevail against them. (John 8:12)
4. I command every evil association or gang targeting my children to be scattered and defeated, in Jesus' name. (Psalm 68:1)
5. I declare that my children are surrounded by angelic protection wherever they go, shielding them from harm. (Psalm 34:7)

6. I break and nullify every curse or negative influence that may be operating in the lives of my children, in the powerful name of Jesus. (Galatians 3:13)
7. I release the power of the Holy Spirit upon my children, enabling them to discern and avoid any dangerous situation on the streets. (John 16:13)
8. I pray that godly mentors and role models be placed in the lives of my children, guiding them away from the influence of the streets. (Proverbs 13:20)
9. I declare that the fear of the Lord surrounds my children, leading them to make wise choices and avoiding the traps of the enemy. (Proverbs 1:7)
10. I bind every spirit of addiction or substance abuse that may try to entice my children on the streets, and I command them to be free in Jesus' name. (Galatians 5:1)
11. I decree that the purposes and destiny of my children shall not be hindered or derailed by any spirit of the street, in the name of Jesus. (Jeremiah 29:11)
12. I plead the blood of Jesus over my children's minds, protecting them from negative influences and deception on the streets. (Revelation 12:11)
13. I pray for divine wisdom and discernment for my children, so they can navigate the streets with godly insight and avoid danger. (James 1:5)

14. I break and demolish every stronghold that the spirit of the street has established in the lives of my children, by the power of Jesus' name. (2 Corinthians 10:4)
15. I declare that my children are more than conquerors through Christ Jesus, and no spirit of the street can overcome them. (Romans 8:37)
16. I pray that the love of God surrounds my children, filling their hearts and keeping them away from the lure of the streets. (1 John 4:18)
17. I bind and silence every lying spirit that may try to deceive my children with false promises or allurements on the streets. (John 8:44)
18. I declare that my children are covered by the armor of God, protecting them from every fiery dart of the enemy on the streets. (Ephesians 6:11)
19. I break every generational curse that may be operating in my family, affecting my children's lives and attracting the spirit of the street. (Exodus 20:5)
20. I release God's favor upon my children, opening doors of opportunity and protection, and closing doors to any harm or danger on the streets. (Psalm 5:12)
21. I decree that my children will be a light in the midst of darkness on the streets, influencing others for the kingdom of God. (Matthew 5:14)

22. I declare that my children have a sound mind and make wise decisions, resisting any pressure or temptation from the spirit of the street. (2 Timothy 1:7)
23. I pray for divine guidance and direction for my children, leading them on paths of righteousness and away from the paths of destruction. (Psalm 23:3)
24. I break and cancel every evil assignment that the spirit of the street has planned against my children, by the authority of Jesus' name. (Isaiah 54:17)
25. I pray that my children will walk in humility and discernment, recognizing the traps and snares set by the spirit of the street. (Proverbs 11:2)
26. I decree that my children will have a heart for justice and righteousness, standing against the injustices and violence on the streets. (Micah 6:8)
27. I release the power of God's Word into the lives of my children, transforming their minds and renewing their thoughts about the streets. (Romans 12:2)
28. I pray for divine connections and friendships for my children, leading them to godly associations and away from harmful influences on the streets. (Proverbs 27:17)
29. I break every assignment of theft, robbery, and violence against my children, declaring that they are protected by the Lord Almighty. (Psalm 91:11)

30. I declare that my children will not be enticed by the glamour and allure of the streets, but they will find their joy and satisfaction in serving God. (1 John 2:15)
31. I pray that my children will have a heart of compassion for those trapped in the streets, becoming instruments of God's love and redemption. (Matthew 9:36)
32. I bind and cast out every spirit of fear that may try to paralyze my children and prevent them from fulfilling their God-given purpose. (2 Timothy 1:7)
33. I pray for divine protection over my children's physical, emotional, and spiritual well-being, guarding them from harm on the streets. (Psalm 121:7)
34. I decree that my children's steps are ordered by the Lord, and they will not stumble or fall into the traps set by the spirit of the street. (Psalm 37:23)
35. I declare that my children are overcomers, and the spirit of the street has no power over them, for greater is He who is in them than he who is in the world. (1 John 4:4)
36. I pray that my children will have a heart of forgiveness, releasing any bitterness or anger that may attract the spirit of the street into their lives. (Colossians 3:13)
37. I break every curse of poverty and lack that may try to entrap my children on the streets, declaring that they are blessed by the Lord. (Deuteronomy 28:2)

38. I declare that my children will walk in purity and holiness, rejecting any form of immorality or impurity that the spirit of the street promotes. (1 Thessalonians 4:7)
39. I pray for divine discernment for my children, enabling them to recognize the tactics and strategies of the spirit of the street and avoid its snares. (Hebrews 5:14)
40. I decree that my children are filled with the Holy Spirit, empowering them to resist the temptations and allurements of the spirit of the street. (Acts 1:8)
41. I break and sever every ungodly soul tie or connection that my children may have formed with individuals influenced by the spirit of the street. (2 Corinthians 6:14)
42. I declare that my children's minds are renewed by the Word of God, protecting them from the lies and deception of the spirit of the street. (Romans 12:2)
43. I pray for divine wisdom for my children, enabling them to make wise choices and avoid dangerous situations on the streets. (Proverbs 2:10-11)
44. I bind and cast out every spirit of rebellion and disobedience that may be attracted to my children through the influence of the street. (1 Samuel 15:23)
45. I declare that my children are hidden under the shadow of the Almighty, and no weapon formed against them by the spirit of the street shall prosper. (Psalm 91:1-2)

46. I pray for godly discernment for my children, helping them to recognize the difference between true freedom and the bondage offered by the spirit of the street. (John 8:32)
47. I decree that my children are filled with courage and boldness, standing against the spirit of the street and declaring the victory of Christ. (Joshua 1:9)
48. I break and destroy every negative influence or ungodly mindset that the spirit of the street may have implanted in the lives of my children. (Romans 12:2)
49. I declare that my children are covered by the precious blood of Jesus, and no harm or danger from the streets can touch them. (Revelation 12:11)
50. I release the power of God's love and grace upon my children, drawing them close to the heart of God and away from the enticements of the street. (2 Corinthians 13:14)

Chapter 13

Beyond the Physical: A Mother's Spiritual War Against the Spirit of Sexual Perversion

In today's world, mothers often find themselves facing various challenges in safeguarding their children's well-being, one of which is the spirit of sexual perversion. This malevolent force seeks to corrupt the innocence of children and destroy their lives. Let's explore the inspiring journey of a warrior mom as she engages in a spiritual battle in the court of heaven against the spirit of sexual perversion, drawing strength from the Scripture.

Understanding the Spirit of Sexual Perversion:

The spirit of sexual perversion encompasses a range of harmful behaviors and desires that deviate from God's design for human sexuality. It aims to exploit and corrupt the gift of sexuality, targeting vulnerable individuals, especially children. The consequences of succumbing to this spirit are far-reaching, leading to brokenness, addiction, and emotional and spiritual damage.

Heavenly Father, I come before you today, seeking your wisdom and discernment to understand the true nature of the spirit of sexual perversion.

Open my eyes to recognize its deceptive tactics and empower me to protect my children from its influence.

Lord Jesus, I declare that I will not be ignorant of the schemes of the enemy. Grant me a deep understanding of your divine plan for human sexuality, that I may impart this truth to my children and equip them with a firm foundation rooted in your Word.

Holy Spirit, I invite you to guide my thoughts and actions as I seek to comprehend the gravity of the spirit of sexual perversion. Help me grasp the devastating consequences it brings upon individuals and society, motivating me to take a stand against it with unwavering resolve.

Heavenly Father, I pray for discernment and sensitivity to detect even the subtle manifestations of the spirit of sexual perversion in the lives of my children. Grant me the grace to address these issues with love, patience, and wisdom, always pointing them towards the path of purity and righteousness.

Almighty God, I declare that you are the ultimate authority over every spirit of sexual perversion. I trust in your power to break the chains that bind individuals and to bring healing and restoration to those affected by its influence. Strengthen me as a warrior mom, that I may boldly confront this spirit and intercede for the liberation of others. In the name of Jesus, I pray. Amen.

The Warrior Mom's Battle:

Recognizing the Threat:
The warrior mom, grounded in her faith and equipped with the Word of God, discerns the lurking danger posed by the spirit of sexual perversion. She understands that her children are prime targets and realizes the urgent need to take action.

Prayer and Intercession:
The warrior mom knows that the battle against spiritual forces requires spiritual weapons. She engages in fervent prayer, seeking God's guidance and protection for her children. Through intercession, she accesses the court of heaven, bringing her petitions before the divine throne.

Arming Herself with Scripture:
The Bible becomes the warrior mom's arsenal, providing her with divine truth, strength, and strategies. She immerses herself in scripture, meditating on verses that combat the spirit of sexual perversion. Verses such as Ephesians 6:12 and James 4:7 empower her to resist the enemy's attacks and protect her children.

Modeling Godly Relationships:
The warrior mom recognizes the importance of modeling healthy relationships within her family. She fosters an environment of trust, open communication, and genuine love, creating a safe space where her children can confide in her and seek guidance.

Heavenly Father, I come before your throne, recognizing the threat of the spirit of sexual perversion targeting my children. I declare that you have entrusted me with the responsibility of protecting their innocence and guiding them in the path of righteousness.

Lord, I seek your divine guidance and wisdom as I engage in this spiritual battle. I declare that your Holy Spirit will empower me to discern and counteract the tactics of the enemy. Help me to navigate the complexities of this issue with grace, love, and truth.

Father, I declare that your Word is my weapon. I arm myself with the scriptures that combat the spirit of sexual perversion. Your promises are my shield, and I stand on verses such as Ephesians 6:12 and James 4:7, knowing that you have equipped me to resist the enemy's attacks and protect my children.

Heavenly Father, I declare that my home is a safe haven for my children. I establish an atmosphere of trust, open communication, and godly love. I pray that my children will feel comfortable confiding in me and seeking guidance, knowing that they are cherished and protected.

Lord, I declare your promises of protection over my children. According to Matthew 18:10, I believe that your angels are watching over them. I pray that you surround my children with a hedge of divine protection, guarding them against the influence and allure of sexual perversion. Give them discernment to make wise choices and the strength to resist temptation. In the mighty name of Jesus. Amen.

Biblical References and Promises:

God's Design for Sexuality:
Genesis 1:27 affirms that God created humanity in His own image, male and female. The warrior mom teaches her children about the beauty and sanctity of God's design for sexuality, instilling in them a solid foundation of biblical values.

Protecting Innocence:
Jesus highlights the importance of protecting children in Matthew 18:6, emphasizing the severity of causing them to stumble. The warrior mom shields her children from harmful influences, monitoring their media consumption and educating them about appropriate boundaries.

Praying for Protection:
The warrior mom finds solace in Jesus' promise of protection in Matthew 18:10, knowing that angels are assigned to watch over her children. She prays daily, invoking God's shield of divine protection and dispatching His angels to safeguard her precious ones.

Overcoming Temptation:
The apostle Paul assures believers in 1 Corinthians 10:13 that God provides a way of escape from temptation. The warrior mom equips her

children with knowledge and discernment, empowering them to resist the allure of sexual perversion and make godly choices.

Declaration of God's Design for Sexuality:
Almighty God, I declare that you created humanity in your image, male and female, according to Genesis 1:27. I thank you for the beauty and sanctity of your design for sexuality. I pray that you will help me teach my children about your divine plan, instilling in them a deep understanding and respect for their bodies and the gift of sexuality. Protect them from the distortions and perversions of the world, that they may embrace and live out your holy design for their lives.

Declaration of Protection for Innocence:
Heavenly Father, I stand firm on your promise in Matthew 18:6, where Jesus warns about causing children to stumble. I pray for a hedge of protection around my children, guarding their innocence and shielding them from the corrupting influences of the spirit of sexual perversion. Strengthen them to discern right from wrong, enabling them to make wise choices that preserve their purity. Grant them the courage to resist temptation and walk in righteousness, even in the face of societal pressures.

Declaration of Angelic Guard:
Lord, I lift up my children to you, knowing that according to Matthew 18:10, angels are assigned to watch over them. I declare that your mighty angels encamp around them, providing constant protection from any harm

or spiritual attack. I pray that you will dispatch your angels to stand as a barrier against any form of sexual perversion that seeks to infiltrate their lives. May your angelic presence bring peace, strength, and discernment to my children, guiding them away from the snares of the enemy.

Declaration of Overcoming Temptation:
Heavenly Father, I declare your promise from 1 Corinthians 10:13, that you provide a way of escape from temptation. I pray that you would grant my children the strength and wisdom to recognize and resist the allure of sexual perversion. Equip them with discernment, that they may navigate through the challenges of this world with purity and integrity. Fill their hearts with a love for your Word and a desire to obey your commands, enabling them to overcome temptation and walk in righteousness.

Declaration of Renewed Minds:
Gracious Father, I lift up my children's minds to you, recognizing the importance of renewing their thoughts and beliefs. According to Romans 12:2, I declare that you have the power to transform their minds, helping them discern what is good and pleasing to you. I pray that you will cleanse their minds from the lies and distortions of the spirit of sexual perversion, filling them with truth, purity, and a deep understanding of your Word. Let their thoughts be guided by your principles and their hearts anchored in your love, that they may live according to your perfect plan.

Seeking Support and Guidance:

Building a Community:

The warrior mom understands the importance of seeking support from like-minded individuals. She surrounds herself with a community of fellow believers who can provide encouragement, prayer, and practical advice in navigating this spiritual battle.

Seeking Professional Help:

Recognizing the complexity and gravity of the issue, the warrior mom seeks professional guidance when necessary. She understands that mental health professionals, pastors, and counselors can offer additional support in addressing the aftermath of any encounters with the spirit of sexual perversion.

Heavenly Father, I come before you with a humble heart, recognizing that I cannot face the battles of protecting my children against the spirit of sexual perversion alone. I declare that I will seek and embrace the support of a godly community that will uplift and strengthen me in this journey.

Lord, I thank you for the gift of wise counsel and guidance. I declare that I will actively seek professional help and advice when needed, understanding that mental health professionals, pastors, and counselors can provide invaluable support in addressing the aftermath of encounters with the spirit of sexual perversion.

Gracious God, I declare that you have placed divine connections in my life. I proclaim that I will surround myself with fellow believers who share my commitment to protecting our children's innocence. Together, we will uplift, encourage, and pray for one another, knowing that in unity, we find strength and wisdom.

Heavenly Father, I declare that I will not allow shame or fear to hinder me from reaching out for support. I surrender any feelings of inadequacy or self-reliance and choose to embrace the vulnerability of seeking help. I trust that you will guide me to the right people and resources, equipping me with the wisdom needed to navigate this battle.

Lord, I declare that I will be transparent and open with those I trust, sharing my struggles and concerns. I will not bear this burden alone, but instead, I will lean on others for support and guidance. I trust that as I open my heart and seek assistance, you will provide the wisdom and discernment necessary to protect my children and guide them on the path of purity and righteousness. In Jesus' mighty name. Amen.

The battle against the spirit of sexual perversion is an ongoing struggle, particularly for mothers who carry the responsibility of safeguarding their children. However, the warrior mom, fortified by her faith and armed with the Word of God, stands firm in the court of heaven, pleading for divine protection and intervention. Through prayer, biblical guidance, and building a supportive community, she fights valiantly for the well-being and purity of her children. As warrior moms rise up, empowered by their faith and love for their children, they become powerful agents of change in a world plagued by sexual perversion, demonstrating the strength and unwavering commitment that comes from the heart of a mother.

"Pray in the language of heaven (Pray in tongues) for at least 10 minutes as you enter into the court of heaven to plead you case; if you cannot pray in tongues, enter His court with praise and worship for at least 10 minutes before you plead your case."

Warfare Prayers:

1. Heavenly Father, I declare that my children are covered by the blood of Jesus, and I stand as a warrior mom to protect them from the spirit of sexual perversion. (Ephesians 1:7)
2. Lord, I plead the blood of Jesus over the minds, hearts, and bodies of my children, guarding them against any influence or temptation of sexual perversion. (Revelation 12:11)
3. I decree that my children are surrounded by angelic protection, keeping them safe from the attacks of the enemy in the realm of sexual perversion. (Psalm 34:7)
4. Father, I break and destroy every generational curse of sexual perversion that may have been passed down in our family line, setting my children free in Jesus' name. (Galatians 3:13-14)
5. I declare that the power of God's truth and righteousness surrounds my children, shielding them from the lies and deception of the spirit of sexual perversion. (Psalm 5:12)

6. Lord, I pray that You would give my children discernment to recognize and reject any form of sexual perversion that may be presented to them, granting them a heart that desires purity. (Proverbs 2:11-12)
7. I rebuke every demonic influence that seeks to infiltrate the minds and hearts of my children with thoughts and desires contrary to your will, O Lord. (2 Corinthians 10:5)
8. Father, I declare that my children are filled with the Holy Spirit, who empowers them to overcome the spirit of sexual perversion and live a life pleasing to you. (Ephesians 5:18)
9. I bind every demonic spirit assigned to attack my children through pornography, sexual exploitation, or any other form of sexual perversion, rendering them powerless. (Matthew 18:18)
10. Lord, I pray for a hedge of protection around my children's friendships and relationships, that they may be surrounded by godly influences that steer them away from sexual perversion. (Proverbs 13:20)
11. I declare that the minds of my children are renewed by the Word of God, transforming them, and guiding them away from the allure of sexual perversion. (Romans 12:2)
12. Heavenly Father, grant my children strength to resist and flee from any situation or temptation that may lead them into the trap of sexual perversion. (1 Corinthians 10:13)
13. I command every demonic stronghold promoting sexual perversion in the media, internet, and entertainment industry to be

dismantled and rendered ineffective in the lives of my children. (Ephesians 6:12)

14. Lord, I pray for divine wisdom and understanding to be imparted to my children, enabling them to discern and reject any form of sexual perversion disguised as freedom or acceptance. (Proverbs 2:6-7)
15. I proclaim that my children are vessels of honor, dedicated to the Lord and set apart from the influence of sexual perversion. (2 Timothy 2:21)
16. Father, I pray that you would strengthen the bond between my children and their siblings, creating a protective shield against any attempt to introduce sexual perversion into their relationships. (Ecclesiastes 4:12)
17. I declare that my children are a light in this world, exposing the works of darkness, including the spirit of sexual perversion. (Matthew 5:14-16)
18. Lord, I bind every spirit of shame and guilt that may try to entangle my children in the chains of sexual sin, and I release the freedom and forgiveness found in Christ Jesus. (Romans 8:1)
19. I speak restoration and healing into any wounded areas of my children's lives caused by exposure to sexual perversion, believing that you will make all things new. (Isaiah 61:3)
20. I pray that my children would develop a deep reverence for their bodies as temples of the Holy Spirit, guarding them against any defilement caused by sexual perversion. (1 Corinthians 6:19-20)

21. I declare that my children will not be swayed by the distorted views of sexuality prevalent in our society, but they will hold fast to the biblical truth that honors God's design. (Genesis 1:27)
22. Lord, I pray for godly mentors and leaders to arise in the lives of my children, guiding them towards purity and righteousness, and protecting them from the spirit of sexual perversion. (Titus 2:7-8)
23. I bind every spirit of confusion and distortion that may try to deceive my children about their gender identity or sexual orientation, declaring that they will embrace their true identity as fearfully and wonderfully made by God. (Psalm 139:14)
24. Heavenly Father, I release the power of your love and grace into the lives of my children, knowing that your perfect love casts out all fear, including the fear of falling into sexual perversion. (1 John 4:18)
25. I declare that my children will have open and honest communication with me, allowing us to address any struggles or temptations related to sexual perversion and find strength and support together. (Proverbs 15:22)
26. Lord, I pray that my children will develop healthy boundaries in their relationships, enabling them to protect themselves from any form of manipulation or coercion that may lead to sexual perversion. (Proverbs 4:23)
27. I declare that the fruit of the Spirit, including self-control, will flourish in the lives of my children, empowering them to resist the allure of sexual perversion. (Galatians 5:22-23)

28. I pray that my children would have a deep understanding of the sanctity of marriage and the beauty of sexual intimacy within the boundaries of a godly covenant, guarding them against the counterfeit pleasures of sexual perversion. (Hebrews 13:4)
29. Lord, I ask that you cleanse my children's minds from any impure thoughts or imaginations, filling their hearts and minds with things that are true, noble, pure, and praiseworthy. (Philippians 4:8)
30. I declare that my children will not conform to the patterns of this world when it comes to sexual behavior, but they will be transformed by the renewing of their minds according to your Word. (Romans 12:2)
31. Father, I pray for divine intervention in the lives of those who may seek to harm or exploit my children through sexual perversion, asking that you would expose their evil deeds and bring them to justice. (Psalm 37:28)
32. I speak strength and courage into the hearts of my children, enabling them to stand firm against the pressures and temptations of sexual perversion, knowing that greater is He who is in them than he who is in the world. (1 John 4:4)
33. Lord, I pray that my children would develop godly friendships and connections, where they can find support, accountability, and encouragement in their pursuit of purity and righteousness. (Proverbs 27:17)
34. I declare that my children's identities are rooted in Christ, and they will find their true satisfaction, fulfillment, and purpose in Him,

not in the distorted pleasures of sexual perversion. (Colossians 2:10)

35. Father, I pray for the restoration of innocence and purity in the lives of my children, undoing any damage caused by exposure to sexual perversion and filling them with a childlike faith and trust in you. (Mark 10:14)

36. I bind every spirit of addiction and bondage related to sexual perversion, declaring that my children will walk in freedom and deliverance, no longer enslaved by its grip. (John 8:36)

37. Lord, I pray that my children would have a strong sense of self-worth and identity in Christ, guarding them against seeking validation or acceptance through sexual promiscuity or perversion. (Psalm 139:13-14)

38. I declare that my children's bodies are temples of the Holy Spirit, and they will treat themselves and others with respect, purity, and honor, rejecting any form of sexual perversion. (1 Corinthians 6:19)

39. I release the power of forgiveness into the lives of my children, knowing that your grace is sufficient to cover any mistakes or sins related to sexual perversion, and you offer them a fresh start. (Ephesians 1:7)

40. Lord, I pray for supernatural discernment and intuition for my children, enabling them to recognize and avoid dangerous situations or individuals that may lead them into sexual perversion. (Hebrews 5:14)

41. I declare that my children are overcomers by the blood of the Lamb and the word of their testimony, and they will not be defined by any past or present struggles with sexual perversion. (Revelation 12:11)

42. I pray for a spirit of humility and teachability to be upon my children, enabling them to receive godly counsel and correction in the areas of sexuality and relationships, guarding them against sexual perversion. (Proverbs 19:20)

43. I bind every spirit of rebellion and disobedience that may open the door for the enemy's attacks through sexual perversion, declaring that my children will submit to God and resist the devil. (James 4:7)

44. Lord, I pray for divine appointments and encounters for my children, where they can encounter your truth and love, experiencing a transformation that breaks the chains of sexual perversion. (Acts 9:3-6)

45. I speak restoration and healing into the brokenness caused by sexual perversion in the lives of my children, believing that you are the God who makes all things new and can redeem any situation. (Joel 2:25)

46. I declare that my children are vessels of honor, reserved for noble purposes in your kingdom, and their bodies will not be defiled or used for the purposes of sexual perversion. (2 Timothy 2:20)

47. Lord, I pray for divine connections and friendships with other families who share our values and commitment to raising children

free from the influence of sexual perversion, creating a network of support and prayer. (Proverbs 13:20)

48. I declare that my children are filled with the Spirit of wisdom and revelation, enabling them to discern the schemes and strategies of the enemy when it comes to sexual perversion. (Ephesians 1:17-18)

49. I release the power of the Word of God into the lives of my children, knowing that your truth is a lamp to their feet and a light to their path, guiding them away from sexual perversion. (Psalm 119:105)

50. Lord, I surrender my children into your hands, trusting that you are able to keep them from stumbling and present them blameless before your presence with great joy, shielding them from the spirit of sexual perversion. (Jude 1:24-25)

Chapter 14

Spiritual Armory: The Armor of God and How to Use It

As a Warrior Mom, you're engaged in a spiritual battle, and to fight effectively, you need the right armor. In Ephesians 6:10-18, the apostle Paul outlines the armor of God, each piece corresponding to a specific truth about who God is and who we are in Him. Understanding and wielding this spiritual armor is crucial to your role as a defender of your children in the court of heaven.

Firstly, Paul speaks of the "belt of truth" (Ephesians 6:14). In a Roman soldier's armor, the belt served to protect the soldier's lower body and to hold other pieces of the armor together. The belt of truth signifies the importance of God's truth in our spiritual warfare. As a Warrior Mom, you're called to gird yourself with the truth of God's Word, allowing it to guide your decisions, your actions, and your prayers for your children. The truth also exposes the lies of the enemy, protecting your children from deception.

Next is the "breastplate of righteousness" (Ephesians 6:14). The breastplate protects the heart and vital organs. Righteousness, right standing with God through Jesus Christ, guards our hearts against accusations and guilt. As you stand in righteousness, not based on your merit but on Christ's, you can confidently intercede for your children, secure in your position before God.

Paul then mentions "feet fitted with the readiness that comes from the gospel of peace" (Ephesians 6:15). This speaks of a readiness to proclaim the good news of Jesus Christ, which brings peace. In your spiritual warfare, you bring the peace of God into your children's lives, declaring the gospel's transforming power over them.

The "shield of faith" (Ephesians 6:16) is our defense against the enemy's fiery darts – doubts, fears, and lies. Your faith in God's character, His Word, and His promises act as a protective shield for your children, extinguishing the enemy's attacks.

The "helmet of salvation" (Ephesians 6:17) safeguards our minds. Understanding and embracing the reality of salvation protect our minds from doubt, despair, and hopelessness. Your assurance of salvation and eternal life in Christ is a source of hope for your children, a beacon of light in their darkest times.

The "sword of the Spirit, which is the word of God" (Ephesians 6:17), is the only offensive weapon mentioned in the list. It's a tool for both defense and offense. As a Warrior Mom, wielding the Word of God in your prayers cuts through enemy lies, brings spiritual breakthroughs, and declares God's promises over your children's lives.

Lastly, Paul exhorts us to "pray in the Spirit on all occasions" (Ephesians 6:18). Prayer is our communication line with the Commander of our heavenly army. In prayer, we receive divine strategies, strength, and encouragement. Your prayers for your children are crucial in the spiritual battle, connecting them with God's power and will.

Each piece of the armor is vital, and together they provide complete coverage. But putting on the armor is not a one-time event; it's a daily, intentional practice. It involves immersing yourself in God's truth, walking in His righteousness, proclaiming His gospel, exercising faith, embracing salvation, wielding His Word, and engaging in prayer.

As a Warrior Mom, you're not just fighting for your children; you're fighting with divine weaponry. The armor of God is your spiritual gear, enabling you to stand your ground, resist the enemy, and see victory in the court of heaven for your children. Remember, your victory is not based on your strength but on the One who has already overcome the world (John 16:33). Stand firm then, with the belt of truth buckled around your waist, the breastplate of righteousness in place, and with your feet fitted with the readiness that comes from the gospel of peace. In addition to all this, take up the shield of faith, with which you can extinguish all the flaming arrows of the evil one. Take the helmet of salvation and the sword of the Spirit, which is the word of God. As you fully embrace and utilize these divine tools, you step into the fullness of your calling as a Warrior Mom, standing in the gap and defending your children in the court of heaven.

"Pray in the language of heaven (Pray in tongues) for at least 10 minutes as you enter into the court of heaven to plead you case; if you cannot pray in tongues, enter His court with praise and worship for at least 10 minutes before you plead your case."

Warfare Prayers:

1. Heavenly Father, I declare that I am strong in the Lord and in the power of His might, putting on the whole armor of God to stand against the enemy's schemes.
2. I put on the belt of truth and declare that I will walk in integrity and discernment, resisting the lies and deceptions of the enemy.
3. I put on the breastplate of righteousness, declaring that my heart is protected by the righteousness of Christ, and I stand in His grace.
4. I put on the shoes of the gospel of peace, ready to share the good news of Jesus Christ and bring His peace wherever I go.
5. I take up the shield of faith and declare that I will extinguish every fiery dart of the enemy with the unwavering trust and belief in God's promises.
6. I put on the helmet of salvation, declaring that my mind is guarded by the knowledge of Christ and His victory over sin and death.
7. I take up the sword of the Spirit, which is the Word of God, and declare that I will wield it with precision and authority to defeat the enemy's attacks.

8. I declare that I am a prayer warrior, and I will intercede on behalf of my family, covering them with the blood of Jesus and claiming their protection.
9. I declare that no weapon formed against me or my loved ones shall prosper, and every tongue that rises against us in judgment shall be condemned.
10. I rebuke every spirit of fear and declare that I am filled with the spirit of power, love, and a sound mind.
11. I renounce every spirit of doubt and declare that I walk in faith, trusting in God's guidance and provision for every aspect of my life.
12. I bind and cast out every spirit of division and strife, declaring that peace and unity reign in my family and relationships.
13. I declare that I am more than a conqueror through Christ Jesus, and I will not be defeated by the enemy's attacks.
14. I break every generational curse and declare that my family is set free from the chains of the past, walking in the blessings of God's promises.
15. I declare that my children are protected by the angels of God, and no harm shall come near them.
16. I bind every spirit of rebellion and disobedience in the lives of my children and declare that they will walk in obedience to God's Word.
17. I declare that my home is a place of peace and refuge, and the presence of God fills every room, driving out darkness.

18. I break every stronghold of addiction and declare that my family is set free from every bondage, walking in the liberty of Christ.
19. I declare that my marriage is strong and flourishing, and no weapon formed against it shall prevail.
20. I rebuke every spirit of sickness and disease, declaring that divine health and healing flow through my body and the bodies of my loved ones.
21. I declare that my mind is renewed by the Word of God, and every thought that exalts itself against the knowledge of Christ is brought into captivity.
22. I declare that I am a vessel of honor, filled with the Holy Spirit, and equipped to do God's work and fulfill my purpose.
23. I rebuke every spirit of discouragement and declare that I am filled with hope and joy, knowing that God is working all things together for my good.
24. I declare that I am a light in this world, and I will shine brightly for Christ, drawing others to His love and salvation.
25. I thank you, Lord, for the victory I have in Christ Jesus. I declare that I walk in the authority and power of His name, and I will see breakthroughs, miracles, and deliverance in my life and the lives of those around me. In Jesus' mighty name, amen!

Chapter 15

Binding and Loosing: Utilizing Spiritual Authority

The Bible speaks about spiritual authority granted to believers. Matthew 16:19 says, "I will give you the keys of the kingdom of heaven; whatever you bind on earth will be bound in heaven, and whatever you loose on earth will be loosed in heaven." As a Warrior Mom, understanding and utilizing this spiritual authority is critical in defending your children in the court of heaven. This chapter delves into the biblical principles of binding and loosing and how you can use them in your spiritual warfare.

The terms 'binding' and 'loosing' were common in Jewish legal language of the first century. Binding meant forbidding or declaring something unlawful, while loosing meant permitting or declaring something lawful. In spiritual terms, binding involves restricting or hindering the work of evil forces, and loosing involves releasing or permitting the work of God's kingdom.

Firstly, it's essential to realize that your authority to bind and loose comes from Christ. Jesus, who has all authority in heaven and on earth (Matthew 28:18), has delegated this authority to His followers. It's not in your name or strength that you bind or loose, but in the name of Jesus.

When you bind, you are proclaiming a restriction or limitation over the works of darkness. For example, you can bind the spirit of fear that's tormenting your child, the lies the enemy is using to deceive them, or the unhealthy influences drawing them away from God. This is not a physical restraint but a spiritual one, achieved through prayer in the name of Jesus.

To bind effectively, you must be specific. Identify what you're binding – is it a spirit of addiction? A spirit of rebellion? Lies about self-worth? Specificity allows you to address the root issue directly. And as you bind, do so with faith, knowing that Jesus has overcome these forces (1 John 4:4).

Loosing, on the other hand, involves releasing God's power, truth, and blessings over your children. When you loose, you are permitting God's kingdom rule in specific areas of your children's lives. You can loose God's peace over your child's anxious mind, His truth over the enemy's lies, or His joy over their sorrow.

Again, specificity is key. What are you loosing over your children? Is it God's wisdom? His guidance? His protection? Also, remember that what you loose should be in line with God's will and Word. For example, it is God's will that your children walk in truth (3 John 1:4), so you can confidently loose truth in their lives.

A crucial point to remember in binding and loosing is that it is not a magic formula or a guarantee of specific outcomes. Instead, it's a way of aligning with God's authority and will, a way of waging spiritual warfare for your children's spiritual welfare.

As a Warrior Mom, you're called to exercise your spiritual authority wisely and boldly. Don't be daunted by the size of the battle or the strength of the enemy. Instead, remember who fights with you - the King of Kings, the Lord of Lords, the One who has already won the victory. Stand in His victory, utilize the authority He has given you, and wage war for your children's destiny.

In conclusion, understanding and implementing the principles of binding and loosing in your spiritual warfare arsenal is critical. As you bind the forces of darkness and loose the power of God's kingdom, you're actively engaging in the battle, wielding your God-given authority to defend your children in the court of heaven. Remember, the battle is real, but so is the victory in Christ. Stand firm, Warrior Mom. The keys of the kingdom are in your hands, ready for you to bind and loose in the name of Jesus.

> *"Pray in the language of heaven (Pray in tongues) for at least 10 minutes as you enter into the court of heaven to plead you case; if you cannot pray in tongues, enter His court with praise and worship for at least 10 minutes before you plead your case."*

Warfare Prayers:

1. In the name of Jesus, I declare my authority as a warrior mom to bind every spirit of fear and release the spirit of courage and strength upon my family.
2. I bind every assignment of the enemy against my children's physical, emotional, and spiritual well-being. I release the power of divine protection over them.
3. I bind every spirit of rebellion and disobedience in my children's lives. I loose the spirit of obedience and submission to God's Word.
4. I bind every generational curse and stronghold that has been passed down in my family. I loose the power of God's grace and freedom to break these chains.
5. I bind every spirit of addiction that may be influencing my children or loved ones. I loose the spirit of deliverance and freedom upon them.
6. I bind every spirit of sickness and infirmity in the name of Jesus. I loose the healing power of God to restore health and wholeness.
7. I bind every spirit of confusion and doubt that may be hindering my family's faith. I loose the spirit of clarity and faith in God's promises.
8. I bind every spirit of strife and division within my household. I loose the spirit of love, unity, and peace to reign in our midst.
9. I bind every demonic influence over my children's friendships and relationships. I loose godly connections and divine alignments in their lives.

10. I bind every spirit of failure and stagnation that may be hindering my family's progress. I loose the spirit of success and breakthrough upon us.
11. I bind every spirit of financial lack and poverty. I loose the spirit of abundance and prosperity in every area of our lives.
12. I bind every spirit of depression and anxiety that may be attacking my family's mental health. I loose the spirit of joy and peace to fill our minds and hearts.
13. I bind every spirit of witchcraft and divination that may be operating against my family. I loose the power of God's Word and discernment to expose and overcome these influences.
14. I bind every spirit of unforgiveness and bitterness within my family. I loose the spirit of forgiveness and reconciliation to restore broken relationships.
15. I bind every spirit of addiction to technology and media that may be affecting my children's lives. I loose the spirit of balance and self-control in their use of these tools.
16. I bind every spirit of lust and sexual immorality that may be tempting my family. I loose the spirit of purity and self-discipline to guard their hearts and minds.
17. I bind every spirit of spiritual complacency and lukewarmness. I loose the spirit of passion and zeal for God's Kingdom and His righteousness.
18. I bind every spirit of deception and false doctrine that may be deceiving my family. I loose the spirit of truth and discernment to guide us in all things.

19. I bind every spirit of lack and scarcity in our lives. I loose the spirit of abundance and generosity to flow through us, that we may bless others.
20. I bind every spirit of procrastination and laziness that may hinder our productivity. I loose the spirit of diligence and excellence in all our endeavors.
21. I bind every spirit of failure and defeat in our spiritual battles. I loose the spirit of victory and triumph to empower us to overcome every obstacle.
22. I bind every spirit of discouragement and despair that may be attacking our hope. I loose the spirit of hope and restoration to fill our hearts.
23. I bind every spirit of pride and arrogance within my family. I loose the spirit of humility and servanthood to guide our actions and interactions.
24. I bind every spirit of witchcraft and occult practices that may be influencing our lives. I loose the spirit of God's light and truth to expose and break these strongholds.
25. I bind every spirit of death and premature destruction over my family. I loose the spirit of life and longevity to dwell within us, according to God's perfect will.

Chapter 16

Shattering Strongholds: Overcoming Generational Curses

The concept of generational curses comes from several passages in the Bible, including Exodus 20:5, where God says, "I, the Lord your God, am a jealous God, punishing the children for the sin of the parents to the third and fourth generation of those who hate me." It suggests that familial patterns of sin or dysfunction can be passed down through generations. As a Warrior Mom, recognizing and breaking these generational curses can be an important aspect of your spiritual warfare for your children.

Firstly, it's essential to understand what a generational curse is not. It's not a divine punishment that's inevitable or unbreakable. Nor is it a reason to live in fear or shame. As a believer in Jesus Christ, you've been set free from the curse of sin and death (Romans 8:2). No curse is more powerful than the work of Christ on the cross.

However, recognizing the patterns of sin, brokenness, or dysfunction in your family line can help you identify potential spiritual battles for your children. For example, if there's a pattern of addiction, fear, depression, or anger in your family, these could potentially be generational strongholds that need to be broken.

To shatter these strongholds, you must begin with repentance. This involves acknowledging the sin or brokenness and turning away from it. As you repent on behalf of your family line, you are essentially breaking agreement with the sin and the curse associated with it. This act of repentance does not earn salvation or favor (which is freely given through Christ) but opens the door for healing and deliverance.

Next, you need to invite God's healing into the areas of brokenness. This could involve prayer, seeking counsel, or sometimes professional help, like therapy. The aim is to allow God's healing to permeate and restore areas that were once held captive by generational curses.

Following this, you must fill the void left by the broken stronghold with God's truth. For example, if you've broken a stronghold of fear, you need to fill that space with faith and trust in God. Speak God's promises and truths over your life and your children's lives, allowing His Word to reshape your thinking and behavior.

Another vital step in breaking generational curses is to establish new, godly patterns. This involves choosing to walk in obedience to God's Word and setting a new course for your family line. It might include starting new spiritual disciplines, like prayer, Bible study, and worship, that cultivate godliness and spiritual health.

Finally, remember that the process of breaking generational curses is a spiritual battle, which means it involves warfare. You may encounter resistance, setbacks, or counterattacks from the enemy. However, don't be discouraged. As a Warrior Mom, you have divine weapons and authority to break every curse and establish God's blessings for your children's generations.

While generational curses may seem daunting, they're not insurmountable. With understanding, repentance, healing, God's truth, new patterns, and persistent warfare, you can shatter these strongholds and see your children walk in the freedom Christ offers. Remember, it's not by your might or power, but by the Spirit of God (Zechariah 4:6). As you stand in the gap for your children, know that the Lion of Judah, the breaker of every chain and curse, is standing with you. Stand firm, Warrior Mom. Your battle is an opportunity for God's victory to be demonstrated, for the chains of the past to be broken, and for a new, godly legacy to be established.

> *"Pray in the language of heaven (Pray in tongues) for at least 10 minutes as you enter into the court of heaven to plead you case; if you cannot pray in tongues, enter His court with praise and worship for at least 10 minutes before you plead your case."*

Warfare Prayers:

1. In the name of Jesus, I declare that every generational curse over my family is broken and nullified.
2. I renounce and sever all ties with any form of witchcraft or occult practices that have influenced my bloodline.
3. By the power of the Holy Spirit, I demolish every stronghold of addiction and bondage in my family line.
4. I release the blood of Jesus to cleanse and purify every generational curse in my lineage.
5. I take authority over every spirit of infirmity and sickness that has plagued my family, and I command them to leave now.
6. I break every curse of poverty and lack that has hindered my family's prosperity and declare God's abundance over us.
7. I declare that the power of the cross breaks every chain of generational sin in my bloodline.
8. I plead the blood of Jesus over my mind, emotions, and thoughts, dismantling every stronghold of fear and anxiety.
9. I rebuke every spirit of division and strife that has caused discord within my family and declare unity and love in its place.
10. I declare that the generational curse of spiritual blindness is shattered, and my family walks in the light of God's truth.
11. I speak restoration and healing into broken relationships within my family, declaring reconciliation and forgiveness.
12. I take authority over every generational curse of premature death, declaring long life and divine health for my family.
13. I declare that generational patterns of failure and defeat are broken, and we walk in victory through Christ Jesus.

14. I renounce and reject every curse spoken over my family, and I declare that only the blessings of God have power in our lives.
15. I command every generational curse of marital strife and divorce to be broken, and I speak restoration and harmony over marriages in my family.
16. I declare that every generational curse that has affected our spiritual gifts and calling is broken, and we walk in the fullness of our God-given destinies.
17. I release the power of the Holy Spirit to fill every void left by generational curses, bringing wholeness and restoration to my family.
18. I command every spirit of rebellion and disobedience to bow before the authority of Jesus Christ in my family.
19. I break every curse of barrenness and infertility, declaring fruitfulness and multiplication in my family.
20. I declare that generational curses of mental illness and depression are shattered, and we walk in the peace and joy of the Lord.
21. I release God's favor and blessing upon every area of my family's lives, cancelling out every curse that has been spoken against us.
22. I declare that the generational curse of broken dreams and missed opportunities is reversed, and we step into a season of divine open doors.
23. I command every generational curse of unbelief and doubt to be broken, and I declare unwavering faith and trust in God's promises.

24. I renounce and break every curse of generational idolatry and false worship, declaring that we serve the one true God.
25. I declare that my family is a generational legacy of God's grace and mercy, and we will walk in the fullness of His blessings.

Chapter 17

Anointed Declarations:
Speaking Life Over Your Children

The Bible tells us in Proverbs 18:21, "Death and life are in the power of the tongue, and those who love it will eat its fruits." Our words have power, more than we often realize. As a Warrior Mom, one of the key weapons in your spiritual arsenal is your spoken word. This chapter explores the concept of anointed declarations and how you can use them to speak life and blessing over your children.

Anointed declarations are faith-filled words spoken out loud that align with the Word of God. They are not wishful thinking or positive affirmations; they are powerful proclamations that can shape reality. They carry the power of God's Word and are infused with His authority.

The first step in making anointed declarations is immersing yourself in God's Word. The more you know the Bible, the more you understand God's will, His promises, and His truth. This understanding forms the foundation of your declarations. For example, if you know that God's Word says your children are a heritage from the Lord (Psalm 127:3), you can declare that blessing over them confidently.

Next, tailor your declarations to the needs of your children. If your child is struggling with fear, declare God's peace over them. If they are grappling with self-esteem issues, declare God's love and their identity in Christ over them. Make sure your declarations are specific, targeted, and relevant.

When you make these declarations, do so with faith. Believe that what you declare in alignment with God's Word will come to pass. Hebrews 11:1 says, "Now faith is the substance of things hoped for, the evidence of things not seen." Your faith in God's Word activates its power in your life and your children's lives.

Consistency is also critical in making anointed declarations. Don't just speak them once and forget about them. Declare them daily over your children. The constant repetition of God's truth can help to shape your children's thoughts, beliefs, and behaviors.

Finally, remember that your declarations have spiritual implications. When you speak God's Word, you're not just speaking to the natural realm but also to the spiritual realm. Your declarations serve as a form of spiritual warfare, combating the lies and attacks of the enemy and reinforcing God's truth and protection.

Here are a few examples of anointed declarations you can make over your children:

1. "[Child's name], you are fearfully and wonderfully made in the image of God. You are loved, chosen, and precious in His sight (Psalm 139:14; Ephesians 1:4)."

2. "[Child's name], God has not given you a spirit of fear, but of power, love, and a sound mind. You are strong, brave, and secure in Him (2 Timothy 1:7)."

3. "[Child's name], you are the head and not the tail, above and not beneath. God's favor surrounds you as a shield (Deuteronomy 28:13; Psalm 5:12)."

Making anointed declarations is a powerful way to wield the Word of God over your children's lives. As you speak God's truth, you are not just talking about what is, but you are also speaking into existence what can be. You are aligning your children's lives with God's promises, fighting spiritual battles, and shaping their destiny according to God's plans. Stand firm, Warrior Mom. Your words carry life, power, and victory. Let them rise like a mighty roar, echoing God's truth and shattering the enemy's lies. Let your declarations resound in the heavens, bringing down blessings and enforcing God's divine purposes over your children.

> *"Pray in the language of heaven (Pray in tongues) for at least 10 minutes as you enter into the court of heaven to plead you case; if you cannot pray in tongues, enter His court with praise and worship for at least 10 minutes before you plead your case."*

Warfare Prayers:

1. In the name of Jesus, I declare that my children are protected by the blood of the Lamb. No weapon formed against them shall prosper.
2. I break every generational curse and negative pattern over my children's lives. They are set free from any bondage or strongholds.
3. I declare that my children walk in the wisdom and guidance of the Holy Spirit. They make godly choices and are led away from any harmful influences.
4. I speak against any spirit of fear, anxiety, or depression that may try to attack my children. They are filled with peace, joy, and the sound mind of Christ.
5. I declare that my children are surrounded by angelic protection. They are shielded from accidents, harm, and any evil plans of the enemy.
6. I speak against any sickness or disease that may try to afflict my children's bodies. By the stripes of Jesus, they are healed and made whole.
7. I declare that my children have a heart that seeks after God. They have a hunger for His Word and a deep love for Him.
8. I speak against any negative influences or ungodly friendships in my children's lives. They are surrounded by godly friends who encourage and support their faith.

9. I declare that my children excel academically. They have a sharp mind, retentive memory, and a love for learning.
10. I speak against any addiction or bondage that may try to ensnare my children. They are free from the grip of addiction and walk in victory.
11. I declare that my children have a heart of compassion and kindness. They treat others with love and respect, reflecting the character of Christ.
12. I speak against any rebellion or disobedience in my children's lives. They have a heart that submits to authority and walks in obedience to God's Word.
13. I declare that my children have a spirit of perseverance and resilience. They overcome challenges and setbacks, never giving up.
14. I speak against any spirit of laziness or complacency in my children. They are diligent and hardworking, using their talents and abilities for God's glory.
15. I declare that my children are blessed in their relationships. They have healthy friendships, strong family bonds, and experience love in all their connections.
16. I speak against any negative self-image or insecurity that may try to affect my children. They know their worth and value in Christ and walk in confidence.
17. I declare that my children have a heart for missions and evangelism. They impact their world with the gospel of Jesus Christ.

18. I speak against any distraction or hindrance that may keep my children from their divine purpose. They stay focused and aligned with God's calling for their lives.
19. I declare that my children have a heart for justice and righteousness. They stand up for truth and make a positive impact in their communities.
20. I speak against any spirit of pride or arrogance in my children. They walk in humility and embrace a servant's heart.
21. I declare that my children have a spirit of forgiveness and reconciliation. They release forgiveness and experience restoration in their relationships.
22. I speak against any negative words or labels that have been spoken over my children. They are defined by God's truth and walk in their true identity in Christ.
23. I declare that my children have a hunger for spiritual growth. They seek the presence of God daily, growing in intimacy with Him.
24. I speak against any confusion or deception that may try to mislead my children. They have a discerning spirit and are led by the Holy Spirit into all truth.
25. I declare that my children fulfill their destinies and impact the world for God's kingdom. They walk in their anointing and bring glory to His name.

Chapter 18

Guardians of Dreams: Safeguarding Your Child's Destiny

In the Bible, God often spoke to His people through dreams. Think of Joseph, the dreamer whose divine dreams set the trajectory of his life and the future of nations. Dreams are not merely the subconscious mind at work; they can be windows into the spiritual realm and God's divine purposes. As a Warrior Mom, part of your role is to be a guardian of your child's dreams, safeguarding their divine destiny.

To be a guardian of your child's dreams, it's vital to foster an environment where dreams and visions are valued and understood. Encourage your children to share their dreams, and listen attentively when they do. Help them see that God may use dreams to speak to them, guide them, warn them, or encourage them.

Understanding the language of dreams can be a daunting task as it often involves symbolic elements. But you can start by studying biblical dreams and their interpretations. Reading and meditating on biblical accounts like Joseph's or Daniel's dreams can provide valuable insights into how God communicates through dreams.

One key principle is that God's dream messages will always align with His Word. If a dream or its interpretation contradicts the Bible, it's not from God. The Holy Spirit, the Revealer of truth, will guide you and your children into understanding. Pray for wisdom and discernment to interpret dreams correctly and to test them against God's Word.

You also need to protect your child's dreams and destiny from the enemy's interference. The enemy would love nothing more than to sow doubt, confusion, or fear regarding your child's divine dreams. Pray for protection over your child's mind while they sleep. Cover them with the blood of Jesus, and ask for God's angelic forces to guard them.

Responding to your child's dreams is equally important. If a dream gives direction, pray about the steps to take. If it reveals a problem, intercede. If it offers encouragement, celebrate it. Teach your child to respond to God's voice, whether He speaks through dreams, His Word, or other means.

Next, encourage your child to record their dreams. This helps them remember the dreams and observe patterns over time. It can also be a valuable tool for seeing how God has spoken and worked in their lives over time.

Most importantly, pray for your children. Pray that they would have dreams and visions from God. The prophet Joel spoke of a time when God would pour out His Spirit on all people, and they would prophesy, dream dreams, and see visions (Joel 2:28). As a Warrior Mom, you can stand in the gap and pray this promise over your children.

Being a guardian of your child's dreams means encouraging and cultivating an environment where dreams are shared, understood, and valued. It involves providing protection through prayer, teaching your child to discern and interpret, responding appropriately, and maintaining a record. You are not just a protector but a mentor, teaching your child to navigate the spiritual aspect of their lives. This guardianship role is an honor and a responsibility that comes with divine help. As you stand guard over your children's dreams and destinies, know that the Maker of Dreams Himself is with you. He will guide, empower, and use you mightily as you guide your children in the realm of dreams and their divine destinies. Stand firm, Warrior Mom. The dreams of your children are precious seeds of divine destiny, and in your faithful guardianship, they will grow into mighty oaks of righteousness, to the glory of God.

> *"Pray in the language of heaven (Pray in tongues) for at least 10 minutes as you enter into the court of heaven to plead you case; if you cannot pray in tongues, enter His court with praise and worship for at least 10 minutes before you plead your case."*

Warfare Prayers:

1. Heavenly Father, I come before you as a warrior mom, ready to intercede for my child's destiny and spiritual protection.
2. In the name of Jesus, I declare that my child is surrounded by a hedge of divine protection against all evil influences.
3. I decree that no weapon formed against my child's destiny shall prosper, and every tongue that rises against them in judgment shall be condemned.
4. I bind and rebuke any spiritual forces of darkness that seek to hinder or divert my child from their God-given purpose.
5. I break any generational curses or negative patterns that may have been passed down through my family line, declaring freedom and restoration for my child.
6. Lord, I pray for a holy discernment to guide me in recognizing and addressing any ungodly influences that may impact my child's journey.
7. I declare that my child is a vessel of God's light, carrying the presence of the Holy Spirit wherever they go.
8. I speak against any negative labels or limitations that others may try to place on my child, declaring their true identity and potential in Christ.
9. By the authority given to me as a parent, I cancel and nullify any plans of the enemy to harm or hinder my child's destiny.
10. I release God's favor upon my child, opening doors of opportunity and divine connections for them to fulfill their purpose.

11. I pray for divine wisdom and guidance to navigate the challenges and decisions my child may face, empowering them to choose what aligns with God's will.
12. I declare that my child's mind is protected from all forms of deception and lies, and they will have a deep understanding of God's truth.
13. Lord, I pray for a circle of godly friends and mentors to surround my child, influencing them towards righteousness and godly living.
14. I declare that my child's heart is guarded against bitterness, unforgiveness, and any emotional wounds that could hinder their progress.
15. I rebuke any spirit of fear or timidity in my child, declaring a spirit of power, love, and a sound mind to operate in their life.
16. I cover my child in the blood of Jesus, declaring divine immunity from any sickness, disease, or harm that may come their way.
17. I pray for supernatural provision in every area of my child's life, believing that God will meet all their needs according to His riches in glory.
18. I declare that my child will walk in integrity and righteousness, resisting the temptations and pressures of this world.
19. I speak blessings and divine favor over my child's education, declaring that they will excel academically and gain knowledge that aligns with God's truth.

20. I declare that my child's gifts and talents will be fully developed and used for God's glory, impacting others, and fulfilling their purpose.
21. I release angels to encamp around my child, safeguarding them from any physical or spiritual harm.
22. I declare that my child will have a heart for justice and compassion, standing up against injustice and making a positive difference in the world.
23. I pray for a deep hunger and thirst for God's Word to be instilled in my child, that they may grow in spiritual maturity and have a strong relationship with Him.
24. I speak supernatural peace and calmness into my child's life, overriding any anxiety, stress, or confusion they may face.
25. Finally, I thank You, Lord, for the privilege of being a warrior mom, partnering with You to shape and safeguard my child's destiny. May Your will be done in their life, and may they bring glory to Your name. Amen.

Chapter 19

Spiritual Warfare in the Everyday: From Schoolyards to Sleepovers

Spiritual warfare is not limited to extraordinary circumstances or special occasions. It's a daily reality that can occur in the most ordinary places, including schoolyards and sleepovers. As a Warrior Mom, you have the responsibility to equip your children to face these battles with wisdom, faith, and courage.

Let's start with the schoolyard. School is a significant part of your child's life, a place where they learn, grow, and interact with others. It's also a place where they may encounter various challenges, from peer pressure and bullying to academic struggles and identity issues. It's essential to help your children understand that these are not just physical or emotional battles; they can also be spiritual battles.

Teach your children the concept of the Armor of God as described in Ephesians 6:10-18. Break down each piece of the armor—the Belt of Truth, the Breastplate of Righteousness, the Shoes of Peace, the Shield of Faith, the Helmet of Salvation, and the Sword of the Spirit—and explain their significance. For instance, the Belt of Truth can help them stand firm against lies and deception, while the Shield of Faith can protect them from fear and doubt.

Pray over your children before they leave for school. Cover them with the blood of Jesus, and declare God's protection, wisdom, and favor over them. Encourage them to start their day with prayer too, seeking God's guidance and strength.

Now, let's move to sleepovers. Sleepovers can be fun and exciting for children, but they can also be a spiritual battleground. They are often in a different environment, under the influence of different spiritual atmospheres, exposed to various influences. Talk to your children about maintaining their spiritual guard even when they are away from home.

Before a sleepover, pray with your children. Ask God to surround them with His presence and protect them from any harmful influences. Also, empower them to make wise choices and to stand up for their values, even when they're under peer pressure.

Remind them that they can call on the name of Jesus at any time. This name carries authority, and it can bring peace, protection, and clarity in confusing or scary situations. Teach them simple prayers they can pray, like "Jesus, help me," or "Jesus, protect me."

Regularly engage your children in conversations about their experiences both at school and during sleepovers. Ask about their friends, their activities, their feelings, and their challenges. Be a safe space for them to share, without fear of judgment or criticism. These conversations can provide valuable insights into the spiritual battles your children might be facing and how you can pray for them and advise them.

Spiritual warfare can occur in the most ordinary places and situations. As a Warrior Mom, your role is not only to fight for your children but also to equip them to fight their battles. This involves teaching them about spiritual warfare, covering them in prayer, empowering them to stand firm in their faith, and engaging in open, honest conversations with them. This daily spiritual warfare may be challenging, but remember, you are not alone. God, the Commander of the heavenly armies, is with you. He strengthens you, guides you, and fights for you. So, stand firm, Warrior Mom. The battle belongs to the Lord, and victory is assured in Christ.

"Pray in the language of heaven (Pray in tongues) for at least 10 minutes as you enter into the court of heaven to plead you case; if you cannot pray in tongues, enter His court with praise and worship for at least 10 minutes before you plead your case."

Warfare Prayers:

1. Heavenly Father, I declare that I am a warrior mom, empowered by your Spirit to fight spiritual battles on behalf of my children.

2. In the name of Jesus, I take authority over every negative influence that may come against my children's lives.
3. I declare that no weapon formed against my children shall prosper, and every tongue that rises against them in judgment will be condemned.
4. I proclaim that my children are surrounded by the divine protection of God, and no harm shall come near them.
5. Lord, I declare that my children walk in the light and are shielded from darkness and evil influences.
6. I decree that my children have the mind of Christ, and they make wise decisions that align with your will.
7. I command every demonic force or spiritual bondage targeting my children to be broken in the mighty name of Jesus.
8. I declare that my children are filled with the Holy Spirit and operate in the gifts and fruit of the Spirit.
9. Lord, I declare that my children are overcomers, and they have victory over every challenge they face.
10. I bind the spirit of fear, anxiety, and depression in the lives of my children and release the peace of God that surpasses all understanding.
11. I declare that my children are strong and courageous, and they walk in boldness and confidence.
12. I command every negative influence from peers or society to be nullified, and I release godly friendships and positive relationships into their lives.

13. I proclaim that my children have a heart for righteousness and a love for God's Word, and they are guided by truth and discernment.
14. Lord, I declare that my children's hearts are protected from the lure of sin and they have a genuine desire to live a holy and blameless life.
15. I declare that my children have a hunger for prayer and intimacy with God, and they cultivate a personal relationship with Him.
16. I bind every spirit of rebellion and disobedience in the lives of my children and release a spirit of submission and obedience to authority.
17. I declare that my children are not influenced by the ways of the world, but they are transformed by the renewing of their minds.
18. I proclaim that my children are equipped with the whole armor of God, and they stand firm against the schemes of the enemy.
19. I command every door of temptation and deception to be closed in the lives of my children, and I release godly wisdom and discernment upon them.
20. I declare that my children are blessed in their studies and academic pursuits, and they excel in their education.
21. I decree that my children have a heart for justice and compassion, and they stand up against injustice and make a positive impact in the world.
22. I declare that my children are anointed for their future, and they walk in the purpose and destiny that God has ordained for them.

23. I command every generational curse or negative pattern in my family bloodline to be broken, and I release the blessings of God upon my children.
24. I proclaim that my children are surrounded by godly mentors and role models who guide and inspire them in their spiritual growth.
25. Lord, I thank you for the victory that is already won in the spiritual realm, and I declare that my children are safe and secure in Your loving care.

Chapter 20

The Power of Forgiveness: Releasing Your Child from Wounds

Forgiveness is a potent weapon in spiritual warfare. The enemy often uses unforgiveness as a foothold, causing deep wounds, bitterness, and even physical and emotional illness. As a Warrior Mom, one of your most critical roles is to help your child navigate the process of forgiveness, thereby releasing them from the chains of hurt, resentment, and anger.

Firstly, it's vital to understand the biblical concept of forgiveness. It's not about forgetting the harm or denying the pain. Instead, it's a deliberate decision to release the offender from the debt they owe you, just as God forgave us our debts through Jesus Christ (Colossians 3:13).

One of the ways you can introduce your child to forgiveness is by modeling it in your life. Children often learn more from what they observe than what they are told. Let them see you forgiving others, and openly share about times when you had to forgive. Share not just about the struggle but also the peace, freedom, and healing that came through forgiveness.

Another way to guide your child towards forgiveness is through conversation and prayer. When your child is hurt, listen empathetically to their feelings. Acknowledge the pain and validate their emotions. Then gently steer the conversation towards forgiveness. Explain that holding onto unforgiveness hurts them more than the offender, and it gives the enemy a foothold in their life.

Pray with your child, leading them to express their pain to God and to forgive the person who hurt them. Prayers don't need to be complicated. They can be as simple as, "God, I'm hurt by what (name) did to me. But I choose to forgive (name) and release them from their debt. Please heal my heart and fill me with your peace."

But what if the hurt is deep and the wound severe? In such cases, it may be appropriate to seek help from a trusted Christian counselor or pastor who can guide your child through a process of inner healing. Remember, forgiveness is a journey, not a one-time event. It may take time for your child to fully release the hurt and the offender.

At times, your child might be the one needing forgiveness. Encourage them to admit their wrong, ask for forgiveness, and make things right, if possible. This can be a difficult but valuable lesson in humility, responsibility, and restoration.

Finally, it's crucial to teach your child about God's forgiveness. Assure them that no matter what they do, God is always ready to forgive them if they come to Him with a repentant heart (1 John 1:9). God's forgiveness is unconditional and complete, and it brings redemption, restoration, and peace.

Forgiveness is a vital element in spiritual warfare. It releases your child from the chains of bitterness and resentment and disarms the enemy. As a Warrior Mom, your role is to guide your child on this journey of forgiveness, through modeling, conversation, prayer, and seeking help when needed. Remember, every step towards forgiveness is a step towards healing and freedom. So, stand firm, Warrior Mom. Lead your child into the freedom of forgiveness, and watch as God turns their wounds into beautiful scars of grace.

> *"Pray in the language of heaven (Pray in tongues) for at least 10 minutes as you enter into the court of heaven to plead you case; if you cannot pray in tongues, enter His court with praise and worship for at least 10 minutes before you plead your case."*

Warfare Prayers:

1. Heavenly Father, I come before you as a warrior mom, interceding for my child. I declare that I am empowered by your Spirit to wage war on their behalf.
2. In the name of Jesus, I break and sever every negative influence and stronghold that has wounded my child's heart, mind, and soul.

3. I declare that forgiveness is a weapon of warfare, and I choose to forgive anyone who has hurt my child, releasing them from the power of bitterness and resentment.
4. Lord, I renounce any generational curses or patterns of hurt that may be affecting my child. I declare that they are free from the chains of the past.
5. By the blood of Jesus, I cancel every assignment of the enemy against my child's life. I declare that they are protected and shielded from all harm.
6. I declare that the power of God's love surrounds my child, casting out fear and insecurity. They are embraced by your perfect love, Lord.
7. I speak healing and restoration into every wound my child has experienced. I declare that they are being made whole, spirit, soul, and body.
8. I release the power of forgiveness into my child's heart. May they experience the freedom that comes from letting go of past hurts and embracing a future filled with hope.
9. Lord, I ask you to replace any negative emotions and thoughts in my child's mind with your truth and peace. Let their mind be renewed by your Word.
10. I declare that my child is a mighty warrior in the Kingdom of God. They have the authority to overcome every obstacle and walk in victory.

11. I come against every spirit of rejection and abandonment that has wounded my child. I declare that they are accepted and deeply loved by you, Lord.
12. I speak life and purpose into my child's future. May they walk in the calling you have placed upon their life and fulfill their God-given destiny.
13. I release the power of the Holy Spirit to bring conviction and repentance in my child's heart. Let them turn away from any destructive paths and walk in righteousness.
14. I declare that my child's identity is found in Christ alone. They are chosen, redeemed, and set apart for your purposes, Lord.
15. I break the power of any negative words spoken over my child. I declare that their ears are attuned to your voice, and they receive affirmation and encouragement from you.
16. Lord, I pray for divine connections and godly influences in my child's life. Surround them with mentors and friends who will speak truth and life into their journey.
17. I bind every spirit of addiction and bondage that may be trying to ensnare my child. I declare that they are set free and walk in the liberty of Christ.
18. I declare that my child has a sound mind and makes wise choices. They are led by the Holy Spirit and have discernment to navigate through the challenges of life.
19. I release the power of God's angels to guard and protect my child wherever they go. I declare supernatural safety and divine intervention in their life.

20. I declare that my child's heart is open to receive the love and forgiveness of God. Any walls of self-protection or hardness are broken down, and they embrace your grace.
21. I declare that my child's steps are ordered by the Lord. They walk in divine alignment with your plans and purposes, experiencing supernatural guidance.
22. I declare that my child is a vessel of honor in your hands, Lord. Use them for your glory and transform their life into a powerful testimony of your faithfulness.
23. I come against every lie and deception the enemy has planted in my child's mind. I declare that they are filled with the truth of God's Word, and the truth sets them free.
24. I release the power of restoration into broken relationships in my child's life. May they experience reconciliation and healing in their family and friendships.
25. Lord, I surrender my child into your loving care. I trust you to work in their life, bringing forth miracles, breakthroughs, and complete deliverance. In Jesus' mighty name, Amen.

Chapter 21

The Prodigal Child:
Hope and Strategies for Wayward Children

Every Warrior Mom's heart yearns for their children to walk in God's ways and fulfill His purpose for their lives. However, sometimes, despite your best efforts, your child may choose a different path, a path that leads away from God and His plans. This chapter is for Warrior Moms with prodigal children. It aims to provide you hope and strategies to help your wayward children find their way back to the Father's embrace.

Firstly, know this: God loves your child more than you do. He yearns for your child's return even more than you. This profound truth should be the foundation of your hope. The parable of the Prodigal Son in Luke 15 vividly illustrates this. The father in the story represents God, who is always looking out for his lost son, ready to run to him at the first sign of return. Your child may be a prodigal now, but God is actively working to draw them back to Himself.

It's essential to understand that you cannot control your child's choices. This can be a hard reality to accept, but it is crucial in maintaining your sanity and peace. However, you have the power to influence them through your prayers and actions. Here are some strategies you can employ.

1. Unceasing Prayer: Never underestimate the power of your prayers. James 5:16 says that the prayer of a righteous person is powerful and effective. Your prayers can move mountains in your child's life. Pray specifically for your child's heart to turn back to God. Declare God's promises over them. Pray that God will send godly influences into their life.

2. Unconditional Love: Let your love for your child reflect God's unconditional love. Avoid nagging, criticism, or condemnation, as these can push your child further away. Instead, show them love, acceptance, and grace. Your unfailing love could be the very thing that leads your child back to God's love.

3. Model Christ: Live your life in a way that reflects Christ. Show your child what a life surrendered to God looks like. Your consistency and faith could be a powerful testimony to your child.

4. Open Communication: Keep the lines of communication open. Let your child know that no matter what, they can always talk to you. Be a good listener. Avoid jumping to conclusions or offering unsolicited advice. Sometimes, your child needs to know they are heard and understood.

5. Strategic Fasting: Consider regular fasting for your child. Fasting, combined with prayer, can break spiritual strongholds in your child's life.

6. Wisdom in Intervention: There may be times when you need to intervene for your child's safety, such as in situations involving substance abuse or illegal activities. Seek God's wisdom and guidance on when and how to intervene.

Remember, God is a God of restoration and redemption. The story of the Prodigal Son ended with a joyful reunion and a lavish celebration. Hold on to the hope that your child's story can have a similar ending. Until then, stand firm, Warrior Mom. Keep praying, keep loving, and keep hoping. God is on your side, and He is fighting for your child.

> *"Pray in the language of heaven (Pray in tongues) for at least 10 minutes as you enter into the court of heaven to plead you case; if you cannot pray in tongues, enter His court with praise and worship for at least 10 minutes before you plead your case."*

Warfare Prayers:

1. Heavenly Father, I declare that I am a warrior mom, standing firm in faith and taking authority over the spiritual battles concerning my wayward child.
2. In the name of Jesus, I bind every plan and scheme of the enemy that seeks to destroy my child's life and bring them back into alignment with your perfect will.

3. Lord, I declare that your love is greater than any stronghold or addiction in my child's life. I pray that your love will surround and draw them back to you.
4. I declare that my child's eyes will be opened to see the truth and recognize the deception of the enemy. They will have a heart that desires to return to you, Lord.
5. I decree and declare that my child will experience a divine encounter with you, Lord, that will transform their life and set them free from every bondage.
6. By the authority given to me through Christ, I break every chain of addiction, rebellion, and disobedience that holds my child captive. They will walk in freedom and surrender to your will.
7. Lord, I release the power of your Word over my child. Let your truth penetrate their heart, renew their mind, and guide their steps back to you.
8. I declare that my child will be surrounded by godly influences and divine connections that will speak life and truth into their situation.
9. Heavenly Father, I declare that my child will have a divine turnaround. What was meant for their destruction will be turned around for their good and for your glory.
10. I bind and rebuke every spirit of fear, doubt, and hopelessness that tries to hinder my prayers and discourage me. I walk in faith, knowing that you are faithful to fulfill Your promises.

11. I declare that my prayers are powerful and effective. Every prayer I pray for my child's deliverance and salvation will not return void but will accomplish its purpose.
12. Lord, I pray for divine protection over my child's physical, emotional, and spiritual well-being. Surround them with your angels and keep them safe from all harm.
13. I declare that my child will experience a supernatural peace that surpasses all understanding, even in the midst of their struggles. your peace will guard their hearts and minds.
14. I declare that my child will have a softened heart and a spirit of humility. They will recognize their need for you and willingly turn to you for forgiveness and restoration.
15. I declare that every generational curse and pattern of rebellion in my family line is broken through the power of Jesus' blood. My child will walk in a new legacy of faith and obedience.
16. Lord, I declare that my child will have godly mentors and counselors who will speak wisdom and guidance into their life. They will be surrounded by people who will encourage their spiritual growth.
17. I declare that my prayers are aligned with your will, Lord. I surrender my desires and trust in your perfect timing and plan for my child's life.
18. I bind the spirit of confusion and declare a spirit of clarity and discernment over my child's mind. They will make wise choices and discern between truth and lies.

19. I declare that my child will have a hunger and thirst for righteousness. They will seek after you wholeheartedly and find their satisfaction in you alone.
20. Lord, I pray for divine interventions and divine appointments in my child's life. You will orchestrate circumstances that lead them back to you and restore their relationship with you.
21. I declare that my child will have a spirit of repentance. They will turn away from their sinful ways and turn their heart towards you, Lord.
22. I declare that my child will be a vessel of your love and grace, sharing their testimony of deliverance and redemption with others who are lost and searching for hope.
23. I declare that my child will walk in their God-given purpose and fulfill the destiny you have ordained for their life. Every setback will be turned into a setup for a greater comeback.
24. Lord, I declare that my child's prodigal journey will become a testimony of your faithfulness and restoration. Their life will be a living testament to your saving power.
25. I declare that as a warrior mom, I will not grow weary in praying and interceding for my child. I will continue to stand in faith, trusting that you are working behind the scenes, bringing about their deliverance and salvation. In Jesus' name, Amen.

Chapter 22

Divine Wisdom:
Guiding Your Children through Life's Challenges

One of the most rewarding and challenging roles you occupy as a mother is to guide your children through life's many obstacles. From their first steps to their first heartbreak, from choosing a career to establishing their own families, your children will face numerous hurdles. These moments not only shape them but also provide valuable opportunities for you to impart wisdom and guidance.

But where does this wisdom originate? As a Warrior Mom, you understand that wisdom is more than mere knowledge or understanding. True wisdom is divine, stemming from God Himself. James 1:5 says, "If any of you lacks wisdom, you should ask God, who gives generously to all without finding fault, and it will be given to you." This divine wisdom is indispensable in guiding your children through the labyrinth of life's challenges.

Let's discuss some ways you can utilize divine wisdom to navigate various stages and aspects of your child's life.

Infancy and Early Childhood

In this stage, your child's mind is like a sponge, absorbing everything around them. The seeds you sow now, both physically and spiritually, will influence their growth and development. Divine wisdom can help you establish a nurturing and godly environment. Pray for wisdom in choosing the right words and actions in their presence and make prayer and reading the Bible regular family activities.

Adolescence

Adolescence is a tumultuous period filled with physical, emotional, and social changes. Your child will grapple with issues of identity, independence, and peer pressure. This is when they might start to question their faith or push boundaries. Divine wisdom is crucial in guiding your child during this stage. Remain patient and understanding and respond with love and grace when they make mistakes. Encourage open conversations about their doubts and struggles. Pray for wisdom in guiding them towards God's truths and not the world's deception.

Young Adulthood

As your child transitions into adulthood, they face significant decisions about their education, career, relationships, and life path. Divine wisdom will allow you to guide but not control, to advise but not insist. Respect their growing independence but remain a source of godly wisdom and counsel. Support them in their decisions, reminding them to seek God's will above all.

Times of Crisis

Life inevitably brings moments of crisis and sorrow. During such times, your child may feel lost, scared, or alone. Your role as a Warrior Mom is not to eliminate all of your child's pain - that's impossible. Instead, you're called to comfort, to stand alongside them, and to point them toward the Healer. Use divine wisdom to guide your responses, ensuring they're filled with empathy, compassion, and faith.

Encouraging their Spiritual Growth

Throughout all stages of life, your most important task is to guide your child's spiritual growth. Divine wisdom can help you model a vibrant relationship with God, foster a love for His Word, and instill godly values. Pray for wisdom to lead by example, to correct with love, and to encourage their personal relationship with God.

As you seek to guide your children through life's challenges, remember these three key principles:

1. Prayer is Essential: Always pray for your children and for the wisdom to guide them. Prayer invites God into your challenges, seeking His power and perspective.

2. Love is Fundamental: Love your children as God loves them. This love is unconditional, patient, and kind. It comforts, forgives, and hopes.

3. Trust in God is Imperative: Trust that God loves your children and has a perfect plan for them. Release them into His care and trust Him for their future.

So, being a Warrior Mom is not a call to perfection but a call to reliance upon God. It's an invitation to tap into the divine wisdom available to you through prayer, scripture, and the indwelling Holy Spirit. It's about standing in the gap for your children, fighting spiritual battles on their behalf, and guiding them through life's challenges toward the love and purposes of God.

> *"Pray in the language of heaven (Pray in tongues) for at least 10 minutes as you enter into the court of heaven to plead you case; if you cannot pray in tongues, enter His court with praise and worship for at least 10 minutes before you plead your case."*

Warfare Prayers:

1. Heavenly Father, I thank you for the privilege of being a warrior mom, standing in the gap for my children.

2. I declare that my children are covered by the blood of Jesus, and no weapon formed against them shall prosper.
3. I break every generational curse or negative pattern that may try to hinder my children's progress, in the name of Jesus.
4. I declare that divine wisdom is their portion, and they will make wise choices in every aspect of their lives.
5. Lord, I pray for a hedge of protection around my children, guarding them from any harm or evil influence.
6. I decree that my children walk in the fear of the Lord, honoring and respecting you in all they do.
7. I bind the spirit of rebellion, disobedience, and peer pressure that may try to lead my children astray, in Jesus' name.
8. I release the spirit of discernment upon my children, enabling them to distinguish between right and wrong, truth and deception.
9. I declare that my children are filled with love, compassion, and empathy towards others, reflecting the character of Christ.
10. Lord, I pray that my children develop godly friendships that will encourage and support them on their journey.
11. I command every addiction or harmful habit to be broken off my children's lives, in the mighty name of Jesus.
12. I declare that my children walk in divine health and strength, immune to sickness and disease.
13. I bind the spirit of fear and anxiety, replacing it with peace that surpasses all understanding in my children's hearts and minds.
14. I decree that my children excel academically, intellectually, and in every area of their education.

15. Lord, I pray for divine favor upon my children, opening doors of opportunity and success wherever they go.
16. I break the power of negative influences or media that may attempt to distort my children's values and beliefs.
17. I declare that my children have a heart for justice, standing up for what is right and defending the weak.
18. I release the anointing of creativity and innovation upon my children, enabling them to impact the world for your glory.
19. I pray for godly mentors and role models to come into my children's lives, guiding and directing them towards their purpose.
20. I declare that my children walk in integrity and honesty, even in the face of temptation or compromise.
21. Lord, I pray for emotional healing and restoration in any area where my children have been wounded or hurt.
22. I bind the spirit of discouragement and failure, releasing a spirit of perseverance and resilience upon my children.
23. I declare that my children have a heart for mission and evangelism, sharing the love of Christ with those around them.
24. I release the spirit of excellence upon my children, enabling them to pursue greatness in all they do.
25. Lord, I thank you for the privilege of raising my children and declare that they will fulfill the purpose You have for their lives.

Chapter 23

The Joy of Victory:
Celebrating Breakthroughs and Overcoming

As a Warrior Mom, you're well acquainted with the battleground of spiritual warfare. You've invested hours in prayer, spent countless nights interceding for your children, and battled relentlessly in the spiritual realm. It's been a journey of faith, a journey of love, and indeed, a journey of warfare. But it is also a journey of victory. In this chapter, we delve into the joy of victory, the celebration of breakthroughs, and the exhilaration of overcoming.

The Nature of Victory

In the context of spiritual warfare, what does victory look like? It's important to understand that victory in the spiritual realm may not always align with our human concept of triumph. Victory in spiritual warfare isn't necessarily about seeing everything in your life going perfectly or according to your plan. Instead, it is about aligning your will and your children's lives with God's perfect plan.

A victory can be a breakthrough in your child's behavior, a newfound peace in your home, a healing from emotional wounds, or a strengthening of faith. Even small victories, like seeing your child make a wise choice or exhibit a Christ-like attitude, should be recognized and celebrated.

The Joy of Victory

The joy that comes with these victories is profound. This isn't a superficial happiness that fades with changing circumstances. It's a deep, abiding joy rooted in the knowledge that God is working in your children's lives, that your prayers are bearing fruit, and that your spiritual warfare is effective. This joy sustains you, encouraging you to press on, fueling your prayers, and deepening your faith.

Celebrating Breakthroughs

Every breakthrough, big or small, is a testament to God's faithfulness and deserves to be celebrated. These celebrations don't have to be elaborate. It can be a moment of shared praise during family devotion time, a special note in your child's lunchbox, or a private moment of worship in the quiet of your prayer closet.

These celebrations serve three primary purposes:

1. Acknowledgment of God's Faithfulness: Celebrations are a way of giving thanks to God, acknowledging His hand in your victories. They redirect our focus from the struggles to God's faithfulness, keeping us grounded in gratitude and hope.

2. Encouragement for Your Children: Celebrations are a tangible way of showing your children that God hears and answers prayers. It encourages them in their faith and helps them recognize God's work in their lives.

3. Motivation to Continue Fighting: Celebrations remind you of the effectiveness of your spiritual warfare, motivating you to keep fighting, praying, and believing.

The Exhilaration of Overcoming

Overcoming challenges through spiritual warfare is exhilarating. There's a sense of accomplishment, not in your strength, but in the power of God who fought with and for you. It bolsters your faith and builds your spiritual resilience.

Romans 8:37 says, "In all these things we are more than conquerors through him who loved us." This is your identity in Christ. You're not merely a survivor, you're a conqueror. Embrace this identity and allow the exhilaration of overcoming to propel you forward in your journey of spiritual warfare.

Maintaining Perspective

In the midst of celebrating victories, it's essential to maintain the right perspective. All victories are God's work, not ours. It is He who grants us the strength to fight, the wisdom to strategize, and the faith to believe. Every victory is a testament to His power, not our efforts.

Furthermore, remember that spiritual warfare is a continuous journey. There will be more battles to fight, more territories to reclaim, and more victories to celebrate. So, let each victory encourage you, but don't let it make you complacent. Let it rather spur you on to more fervent prayer, deeper faith, and bolder spiritual warfare.

Chapter 24

Discipleship at Home: Nurturing Godly Character in Your Children

As a Warrior Mom, your most crucial battlefield is the home, and your most essential weapon is discipleship. The spiritual formation of your children begins in the home and is significantly influenced by your intentional, consistent efforts to nurture their godly character. This chapter explores how you can disciple your children at home, imparting biblical truths, cultivating a love for God, and nurturing Christlike character.

Defining Discipleship

Discipleship is about training and teaching people to follow Jesus and become more like Him. It involves teaching the Word of God, modeling Christlike behavior, and encouraging a personal relationship with Jesus. Discipleship, especially at home, is more than just teaching your children biblical stories. It's about integrating faith into every aspect of daily life—sharing in God's truth during ordinary routines and life's unexpected moments.

Discipleship and Spiritual Warfare

Discipleship at home is a powerful strategy in spiritual warfare. As you guide your children to know God, love Him, and follow His ways, you're equipping them with the armor of God—truth, righteousness, peace, faith, salvation, and the Word of God (Ephesians 6:14-17). You're fortifying their spiritual defenses and strengthening their offense, preparing them to stand firm against the enemy's schemes and advance the kingdom of God.

Creating a Discipleship Culture at Home

Creating a discipleship culture at home starts with making God's Word the foundation of your family life. This involves:

1. Regular Family Devotions: Spend time together as a family in the Word, prayer, worship, and discussion. Adapt the format and frequency to suit your family's needs and schedule.

2. Integration of Biblical Teachings in Everyday Life: Use daily routines, activities, and conversations as opportunities to impart biblical truths. For example, you can explain the concept of stewardship while teaching your child to save money or demonstrate forgiveness during sibling squabbles.

3. Personal Relationship with God: Encourage each child to cultivate their personal relationship with God through personal Bible study, prayer, and reflection.

4. Service to Others: Teach your children to serve others in love, following Jesus' example. This can be volunteering as a family, helping a neighbor, or simply teaching them to be considerate of others' needs.

5. A Christ-centered Environment: Create a Christ-centered environment in your home. This includes the books, music, movies, and games you allow, the way you celebrate holidays, and the traditions you create.

Teaching the Word

Teaching your children the Word of God is central to discipleship. However, it's not about filling their heads with biblical facts; it's about nurturing a love for the Word, a desire to live by it, and an ability to apply it to their lives.

To teach the Word effectively, consider these strategies:

1. Make it Age-appropriate: Adapt your teaching to your child's developmental stage. Use children's Bibles, storybooks, and age-appropriate Bible study materials.

2. Make it Interactive: Engage your children in the learning process. Encourage questions, facilitate discussions, and do interactive activities that reinforce the lessons.

3. Make it Relevant: Connect the biblical teachings to your child's daily life and experiences. This will help them see the relevance of the Word and motivate them to live by it.

Modeling Christlike Character

Modeling is a potent form of teaching. Your children are watching you, and your actions often speak louder than your words. Modeling Christlike character involves living out your faith authentically, demonstrating the fruits of the Spirit (Galatians 5:22-23), and responding to life's challenges with faith, hope, and love.

Imparting Spiritual Disciplines

Teaching your children spiritual disciplines is an integral part of discipleship. These disciplines include Bible study, prayer, worship, service, and fasting. Start with simple practices suitable for their age and gradually introduce more complex disciplines as they grow.

Dealing with Mistakes and Failures

Discipleship also involves guiding your children in dealing with mistakes and failures. It's about teaching them to repent, seek forgiveness, learn from their mistakes, and depend on God's grace. Remember, it's not about perfection but progression in their journey of faith.

Discipleship at home may seem overwhelming, but remember, you're not alone. The Holy Spirit is your Helper, guiding you and empowering you in this divine assignment. And rest assured, your efforts to disciple your children at home will bear fruit, shaping them into godly individuals and equipping them for spiritual warfare. So, press on, Warrior Mom, in faith, love, and perseverance, nurturing the godly character of your children in the heart of your home.

Chapter 25

Cultivating an Atmosphere of Worship: Praise as Warfare

In the realm of spiritual warfare, worship is a powerful weapon. Worship invites the presence of God into your home, ushers in His peace, and drives out the enemy's influence. This chapter dives deep into cultivating an atmosphere of worship in your home and harnessing the power of praise as warfare.

The Power of Worship

Worship goes beyond singing songs on a Sunday morning—it's an expression of love, adoration, and reverence towards God. It's acknowledging who God is—His nature, attributes, works, and worthiness. It's giving Him His rightful place in our hearts and lives.

Worship has immense power, primarily for three reasons:

1. God Inhabits the Praises of His People: Psalm 22:3 says that God is enthroned in the praises of His people. When you worship, you create a dwelling place for God's presence, where His power, peace, and joy fill your environment.

2. Worship Redirects Our Focus: Worship takes our eyes off our problems and focuses them on God. It reminds us of God's greatness, faithfulness, and sufficiency, which fosters faith and dissipates fear.

3. Worship Confounds the Enemy: Worship is a form of spiritual warfare that disarms the enemy. In 2 Chronicles 20, as Judah worshipped, God set ambushes against their enemies, and they were defeated.

Cultivating an Atmosphere of Worship

Cultivating an atmosphere of worship means intentionally creating a home environment where God is honored, loved, and experienced daily. Here are some ways to cultivate an atmosphere of worship in your home:

1. Make Worship a Lifestyle: Worship should not be a once-a-week event but a lifestyle. Encourage spontaneous moments of worship throughout the day—while preparing meals, driving to school, or before bedtime.

2. Family Worship Time: Establish regular family worship times. This could include singing worship songs, reading scriptures aloud, praying together, or simply being quiet in God's presence.

3. Incorporate Worship in Routines: Incorporate worship into your daily routines. Play worship music during chores, use mealtime prayers to thank God, use drive-time to meditate on God's goodness.

4. Create Worshipful Spaces: Create spaces in your home conducive for worship, like a prayer corner or an altar. Encourage your children to have their personal worship spaces too.

5. Celebrate God's Faithfulness: Regularly recount and celebrate God's faithfulness. Share testimonies, remember answered prayers, and celebrate God's blessings. This cultivates gratitude, a vital aspect of worship.

Praise as Warfare

Praise is a form of worship that involves expressing joyful thanks to God for who He is and what He has done. Praise is a powerful weapon in spiritual warfare.

When you praise God in the face of difficulties, you declare your faith in His power, wisdom, and goodness. It's a defiant act against the enemy, affirming that your hope is in God and not in your circumstances.

Praise also sets the stage for God's intervention. As seen in the story of Jericho (Joshua 6) and Jehoshaphat (2 Chronicles 20), praise can usher in divine intervention, causing walls to fall, and enemies to be defeated.

Leading Your Children in Worship

As a Warrior Mom, one of your roles is to lead your children in worship. Teach them what worship is, why we worship, and how to worship. Model authentic worship, encourage their participation, and nurture their personal worship experiences.

So, cultivating an atmosphere of worship transforms your home into a stronghold of God's presence, a place of peace amidst the storm, and a launching pad for victorious spiritual warfare. So, Warrior Mom, let your home echo with the sounds of worship, for in this symphony of praise, the enemy is silenced, and victory is secured.

Chapter 26

Testimonies of Triumph: Stories of Warrior Moms in Action

In the journey of faith, testimonies are like mile markers. They remind us of God's faithfulness and instill hope for the future. The testimonies of Warrior Moms can inspire, instruct, and infuse strength into other mothers who are fighting their battles. This chapter shares a series of inspiring stories of Warrior Moms, chronicling their struggles, their strategies, and their victories.

Sarah: The Strength in Stillness

Sarah was a single mom working two jobs and juggling the responsibilities of raising her teenage daughter, Grace. She was exhausted, and the strain was starting to show on Grace as well, who was beginning to have difficulties in school.

One day, Grace confided in Sarah about a series of nightmares she had been having. In these dreams, a dark figure loomed over Grace, whispering negative words that magnified her fears and insecurities. Sarah felt a chill run down her spine. This wasn't just a teenage phase; this was a spiritual attack.

Sarah sprang into action. She began to fill her home with worship music and scriptures. She would pray over Grace every night before bed and would often wake up in the middle of the night to intercede on her behalf.

Months passed, and the nightmares began to lessen until they finally stopped. Grace's countenance changed; her grades improved, and peace returned to their home. The victory did not come overnight, but through steadfast prayer, consistent worship, and relentless love, Sarah defeated the enemy's assault.

Elizabeth: Breaking Generational Curses

Elizabeth grew up in a family plagued by alcohol addiction. When she had her son, she made a vow - her child would not fall into the same trap. But as he grew older, she noticed her son, David, showing an unhealthy inclination towards alcohol.

Instead of succumbing to fear, Elizabeth chose to fight. She began to study scriptures about deliverance and freedom from generational curses. Armed with the Word, she engaged in strategic prayer warfare, petitioning God to break the chain of addiction in her lineage.

She engaged David in conversations about her family history, shared scriptures about the importance of sobriety, and prayed with him. She also sought help from her church community, asking them to stand with her in prayer.

Months later, David admitted to his struggle with alcohol and agreed to seek help. Today, David is not only sober but actively helps others overcome their addictions. Elizabeth's faith, perseverance, and strategic prayer effectively shattered a generational stronghold.

Ruth: The Power of a Mother's Proclamation

Ruth's son, Samuel, was diagnosed with autism at an early age. While accepting and loving her son just as he was, Ruth believed that her son's diagnosis did not limit God's plans for him.

Every day, Ruth would lay her hands on Samuel and speak declarations of health, success, and divine purpose over him. She would read him scriptures, telling him that he was fearfully and wonderfully made by God.

While attending to his medical needs, she was relentless in her spiritual warfare, believing that God could do a miraculous work in Samuel's life. And God did.

Samuel began to show significant improvements. He started communicating more clearly, interacting more, and even excelling in certain areas like memory and music. Teachers and therapists were amazed. Ruth's persistent declarations had created an atmosphere of faith that opened the door for a divine turnaround.

Leah: Intercession for a Prodigal

Leah's daughter, Hannah, was a prodigal. She had abandoned her faith and was leading a life that was far from God's best for her. Leah was heartbroken but not defeated.

Every day, Leah would go into Hannah's room, lay hands on her belongings, and pray for her return. She stood on the promise in Isaiah 49:25, proclaiming that the captive of the mighty would be taken away, and the prey of the tyrant would be rescued.

Her prayers were not without opposition. She was often met with resentment and rejection from Hannah. Yet, Leah pressed on, believing in God's promise.

One day, Hannah came home, tears streaming down her face. She had had a dramatic encounter with God that left her desperate to return to Him. Today, Hannah serves alongside her mother in their local church, reaching out to other prodigals. Leah's relentless intercession had called her daughter back from the enemy's grip.

These stories of triumph remind us of the power of a Warrior Mom's prayers. They reveal the potential for victory that lies within every struggle, encouraging us to stand firm, wage war, and not give up. For in each Warrior Mom's battle, God's power is made perfect, His love is made tangible, and His victory is made certain.

Chapter 27

A Mother's Mantle:
Raising the Next Generation of Warriors

Being a mother is more than bearing children and providing for their physical needs. A mother is a protector, a nurturer, and above all, a warrior. She has the mandate to raise not just children, but warriors. Warriors who are ready to defend their faith, stand against the enemy's wiles, and establish God's kingdom on earth. The mantle of a mother is the mandate to raise the next generation of spiritual warriors.

To raise warriors, mothers must first understand what a warrior is. A spiritual warrior is one who stands firm in their faith, battles the enemy's schemes with divine power, and relentlessly pursues God's heart. They are not swayed by the winds of adversity, but they stand strong in the truth, clothed in the armor of God, and empowered by the Spirit.

But how does a mother raise a warrior? It begins with her own transformation. A mother must first be a warrior herself. She must immerse herself in the truth of God's word, engage in persistent prayer, and live a life of faith and obedience. Only then can she model the warrior-like attributes to her children.

A mother's first lesson to her children is often non-verbal. It's in the way she handles adversity, the way she prays, and the way she trusts God in all circumstances. These silent lessons often leave an indelible mark on a child's spirit, instilling in them a resolve to trust and follow God.

Teaching the children about spiritual warfare is critical. Mothers must not shy away from explaining the reality of spiritual battles and the enemy's tactics. This must, however, be done in an age-appropriate manner, ensuring not to instill fear but to build faith. The knowledge of spiritual warfare empowers children to recognize the enemy's tactics and to counter them with the truth.

Prayer is a mighty tool in a mother's arsenal. Through prayer, she can cover her children in God's protection, intercede on their behalf, and call forth their divine destiny. Regular prayer times with children not only strengthen their spiritual defenses but also cultivate in them a lifelong habit of turning to God.

Mothers also have the divine commission to instill in their children a deep love for God's word. The Bible is the sword of the Spirit, an offensive weapon in spiritual warfare. By teaching children to read, understand, and apply the Bible, mothers equip them with the weapon to counter the enemy's lies with truth.

In addition, a mother should foster an atmosphere of worship in the home. Worship realigns our focus on God, strengthens our faith, and confuses the enemy. Encouraging children to engage in personal and corporate worship develops in them a heart that seeks after God.

Moreover, mothers should teach their children about the power of their words. Declarations and proclamations based on God's word have the power to change circumstances, shift atmospheres, and defeat the enemy's plans. Training children to speak life and declare God's promises over their lives prepares them to stand firm in their faith.

Raising warriors also involves teaching children about the power of love and forgiveness. Hatred and unforgiveness are devices the enemy uses to cause division and strife. Mothers must teach their children to choose love over hate and forgiveness over bitterness, thereby denying the enemy a foothold in their lives.

Lastly, cultivating a warrior's mentality in children is about encouraging resilience and perseverance. Life is full of challenges, and spiritual battles can be intense. Teaching children to remain steadfast in the face of adversity, to press on in prayer, and to hold onto God's promises, helps develop in them a warrior's tenacity.

In the end, raising spiritual warriors is about instilling in them a God-centric worldview. It's about teaching them to put God first, to seek His will in all they do, and to fight the good fight of faith. Mothers who successfully pass on this mantle to their children will indeed raise up a generation of warriors, ready to advance God's kingdom and stand firm against the enemy.

The mantle of motherhood is a sacred commission from God. Mothers are not just raising children; they are raising warriors. Warriors who will stand in the gap, fight the good fight of faith, and triumph over the enemy. As mothers embrace this mantle and invest in their children's spiritual growth, they will raise up a new generation of warriors, armed and ready for battle. For in the spiritual realm, every mother is a Warrior Mom, called to raise the next generation of spiritual giants.

Chapter 28

The Power of Unity:
Forming Prayer Groups and Alliances

Unity holds immense power. It amplifies voices, strengthens resolve, and in spiritual terms, can shake the very foundations of the enemy's strongholds. When mothers, these warriors of faith, come together in unity, they form a formidable front, leveraging collective power in prayer, nurturing each other's faith, and uplifting each other in the journey of spiritual warfare. Forming prayer groups and alliances is not just about community; it's about creating an amplified force of intercession and resistance against the spiritual enemy.

Firstly, we should consider the significance of prayer groups in spiritual warfare. In the words of Jesus in Matthew 18:20, "For where two or three gather in my name, there am I with them." There's power in collective prayer, an undeniable presence of God that rests upon a group of believers united in prayer.

A prayer group is not just an assembly of believers; it is a spiritual alliance. An alliance formed not based on common interests or benefits, but on the shared faith in God's power and His promise of victory. In this alliance, the individual spiritual warriors find strength in numbers, their prayers resonating in harmony, creating a symphony of intercession that echoes in the heavens and counters the enemy's schemes.

Forming a prayer group begins with recognizing the need for one. Mothers who have understood the intensity of spiritual warfare and acknowledged their role as prayer warriors often feel a divine calling to connect with others who share the same understanding. This acknowledgment is often the first step in forming a prayer group.

The next step is seeking likeminded mothers. Mothers who are also waging spiritual battles and who understand the value of collective prayer. This seeking can happen within one's existing circle of friends, within a church community, or even in online spaces dedicated to spiritual growth and prayer. Remember, it is the unity of spirit and purpose that matters, not the location or the number of participants.

Organizing the group comes next. Establishing a clear purpose and structure for the prayer group is vital. The group can agree on specific prayer topics or follow a rotation where each member's concerns are prayed for. Creating a comfortable and safe space for sharing is key. It could be a physical location or a virtual space, depending on the group's convenience.

There must be respect for diversity within the prayer group. Different members may have different prayer styles, theological understanding, and personal experiences. It is crucial that the group maintains a spirit of unity amidst this diversity, respecting each other's perspectives, and focusing on the shared goal of intercession.

Consistency is crucial in a prayer group. Regular meetings, whether weekly, bi-weekly, or monthly, help to maintain the momentum and foster a sense of commitment within the group. Consistency also creates a rhythm of prayer, a spiritual discipline that strengthens the individual and the group as a whole.

Leadership in a prayer group is less about authority and more about facilitating. The leader's role is to guide the group in focused prayer, ensure a respectful and supportive environment, and encourage participation from all members. Leadership in a prayer group can also be rotational, allowing each member to take turns guiding the group.

A prayer group is also a platform for mutual encouragement and support. As members share their struggles, victories, and lessons in spiritual warfare, they uplift and inspire each other. This mutual sharing and caring create a strong bond of sisterhood among the warrior moms, a bond that strengthens their resolve in the face of spiritual battles.

Creating alliances with other prayer groups also amplifies the power of intercession. These alliances allow for a larger network of prayer warriors, each group supporting and reinforcing the others. These alliances can also organize joint prayer meetings or intercessory campaigns, uniting their voices in a concerted cry for spiritual breakthroughs.

So, forming prayer groups and alliances is a strategic move in spiritual warfare. It brings together warrior moms in a united front, amplifying their prayers and providing mutual support and encouragement. These prayer groups and alliances embody the power of unity, a power that can shake the enemy's strongholds and usher in divine victories.

As mothers, as warriors, and as members of these prayer alliances, remember this - the enemy may be strong, but the united body of Christ is stronger. In unity, we find strength. In unity, we find power. In unity, we find victory. And this unity starts with each one of us, opening our hearts to others, inviting them into our journey, and together, raising our voices in intercession for our children and the generations to come. Let us be the carriers of this unity, for we are stronger together, and together, we will see the victory.

Chapter 29

Warrior Moms in the Bible: Lessons from the Matriarchs

The Holy Bible is a vast trove of narratives, wisdom, and teachings, but amidst its pages, it houses stories of remarkable women, mothers, who were warriors in their own right. Each of these matriarchs displayed unique qualities, faced unique challenges, and taught us unique lessons that we, as warrior moms of today, can draw upon.

Eve, the mother of all living, was the first woman, the first wife, and the first mother. Her story, though tainted by the original sin, speaks volumes about the heart of a mother. Even after being banished from Eden, Eve didn't succumb to despair. Instead, she brought life into the world, underlining a mother's ability to create, nurture, and give life, even in the midst of desolation. From Eve, we learn the valuable lesson of resilience. No matter the spiritual warfare we face, we can remain resilient, hopeful, and life-giving.

Sarah, the wife of Abraham, teaches us about faith and patience. Despite her advanced years, she believed in God's promise of a child and waited patiently for its fulfillment. Even in moments of doubt, she clung onto hope, eventually giving birth to Isaac, the child of promise. As warrior moms, we too face periods of waiting and uncertainty. Sarah's story encourages us to hold onto God's promises, to trust in His timing, and to maintain our faith, even when circumstances seem impossible.

The story of Jochebed, Moses' mother, is a testament to a mother's bravery and resourcefulness. To save her son from Pharaoh's decree, Jochebed crafted a waterproof basket and set Moses adrift on the Nile. Her brave act not only saved Moses but also set in motion a chain of events that led to Israel's deliverance from Egypt. Jochebed's story inspires us to be brave, resourceful, and willing to take risks for the protection and well-being of our children.

Hannah, the mother of Samuel, was a woman of fervent prayer. In her deep anguish and longing for a child, she poured out her soul before the Lord. She didn't merely pray; she made a vow, dedicating her yet-to-be-born son to God's service. Hannah's prayers were answered, and she was blessed with Samuel, whom she joyfully dedicated to the Lord. As warrior moms, we learn from Hannah the power of fervent prayer and the joy of dedicating our children to God's purpose.

Bathsheba, the mother of Solomon, teaches us about redemption and the importance of wise counsel. Despite the controversy surrounding her entry into David's life, Bathsheba emerged as a key figure in ensuring Solomon's succession to the throne. She offers a lesson in redemption and change, showing us that past mistakes don't define us. Furthermore, her influence on Solomon, reflected in his Proverbs, emphasizes a mother's role in shaping her children's wisdom and understanding.

Mary, the mother of Jesus, is perhaps the most revered mother figure in the Bible. Chosen to bear the Savior of the world, Mary displayed unwavering faith, humble submission, and immense strength. From the manger to the cross, she stood by her Son, sharing in His joys and sorrows. Mary's life teaches us about sacrificial love, courage, and the strength that comes from absolute trust in God.

Each of these biblical mothers offers unique lessons in faith, courage, patience, prayer, redemption, and love. As warrior moms, we can draw from their experiences and their wisdom in our own spiritual battles. Their lives remind us that we are not alone in our struggles; mothers before us have faced challenges, fought battles, and emerged victorious.

So, take heart from these matriarchs. Embrace the qualities they exemplified - the resilience of Eve, the faith of Sarah, the bravery of Jochebed, the fervency of Hannah, the wisdom of Bathsheba, and the humble strength of Mary. For in doing so, we do more than merely read their stories; we carry forward their legacy, embodying their qualities in our lives and in our roles as mothers.

Remember, each battle we face, each prayer we utter, each tear we shed, and each victory we secure, we do not for ourselves alone but for our children and the generations to come. As we draw wisdom from the matriarchs of the past, we also lay the groundwork for the warriors of the future.

Thus, the journey of a warrior mom is not just about the present; it reaches back into the past, gleaning wisdom from those who walked before us, and stretches forward into the future, paving the way for those who will follow. So, rise up, warrior mom, for your journey is significant, your battles matter, and your victories resonate far beyond what you can see.

May these lessons from the matriarchs guide you, inspire you, and empower you in your journey as a warrior mom, as you stand in the gap for your children, fight on your knees, and secure victories in the spiritual realm. For you are not just a mother; you are a warrior, a matriarch in your own right, shaping the present and the future through your prayers, your actions, and your unwavering faith.

Chapter 30

When We Fall: Dealing with Disappointments and Setbacks

As warrior moms, we stand in the spiritual battlefield daily, advocating for our children and our families. We fight valiantly, bravely, tirelessly. But sometimes, despite our best efforts, despite our prayers and our battles, we fall. We face disappointments. We encounter setbacks. These moments, while disheartening, are part of our journey. And as with any aspect of our journey, there are lessons to be gleaned, strength to be gained, and grace to be discovered.

Understanding Disappointments and Setbacks

Disappointments and setbacks are part and parcel of life. They are moments when expectations aren't met, when things don't go as planned. They are stumbles on the path, hurdles in our journey, reminders that we live in a fallen world where perfection remains an elusive goal. As warrior moms, disappointments might look like unanswered prayers, unmet spiritual goals, or struggles in our children's lives that persist despite our earnest intercessions.

These experiences, while disheartening, are not indicators of defeat. Nor are they signs of inadequacy or a lack of faith. Rather, they are moments that test our resolve, our resilience, and our reliance on God. They are instances that strip away our self-sufficiency, reminding us of our dependence on God, pushing us closer to Him, and shaping us more into the image of Christ.

Embracing the Reality of Our Humanity

In the face of disappointments and setbacks, it's essential to remember that we are human. We are not invincible; we are not immune to failures or immune to emotions. We hurt, we grieve, we question, and sometimes, we falter. And that's okay.

God, in His infinite wisdom, created us with a spectrum of emotions. He designed us with the capacity to feel joy and sorrow, triumph and disappointment. In the Psalms, we see a raw and vivid display of emotions, ranging from exuberant joy to deep despair. In Jesus, we see a God who weeps, who feels compassion, who understands our human experience.

Therefore, when disappointments come, it's okay to feel. It's okay to mourn the loss of expectations. It's okay to lament the setback. It's okay to bring our questions, our doubts, our fears before God. He hears. He understands. And He cares.

Leaning Into God's Grace

Disappointments and setbacks, while painful, provide opportunities to lean into God's grace. When we feel the sting of disappointment, when we grapple with setbacks, we are invited to encounter God's grace in profound and personal ways.

Firstly, God's grace meets us in our weakness. In 2 Corinthians 12:9, the Apostle Paul, grappling with his "thorn in the flesh," hears the comforting words of Christ, "My grace is sufficient for you, for my power is made perfect in weakness." In moments of disappointment, in the face of setbacks, God's grace is sufficient. His power is available. His strength is perfected in our weakness.

Secondly, God's grace reassures us of His unfailing love. Romans 8:38-39 reminds us that nothing can separate us from the love of God. No disappointment, no setback, no failure is potent enough to alienate us from God's love. In moments of disappointment, we are still held firmly in the grip of His unfailing love.

Thirdly, God's grace promises us that He is working for our good. Romans 8:28 affirms that "in all things God works for the good of those who love him, who have been called according to his purpose." This includes our disappointments and setbacks. In ways we may not see or understand, God is weaving our disappointments and setbacks into His grand design, bringing beauty out of ashes, and working for our ultimate good.

Responding to Disappointments and Setbacks

While disappointments and setbacks are challenging, they are not insurmountable. The way we respond to these moments can shape our journey, influence our spiritual growth, and impact our effectiveness as warrior moms.

Firstly, acknowledge the disappointment. Ignoring or suppressing our emotions doesn't make them disappear. Instead, it might lead to emotional overload or burnout. So, give yourself permission to acknowledge your feelings, to mourn your losses, to express your heart to God.

Secondly, embrace God's grace. In moments of disappointment, lean into God's grace. Let His grace wash over your weaknesses, your failures, your disappointments. Allow His grace to reassure you of His love, to remind you of His sovereignty, and to reorient you to His purposes.

Thirdly, adjust your perspective. Disappointments and setbacks, while painful, can also be powerful catalysts for growth. They can spur us to reevaluate our expectations, to reassess our strategies, and to realign ourselves with God's will. They can serve as opportunities to deepen our dependence on God, to grow in character, and to mature in faith.

Finally, keep going. Falling isn't the end of the journey. Disappointment isn't the end of the story. With God's grace, we rise. With God's strength, we press on. With God's guidance, we navigate the setbacks, we surmount the disappointments, and we continue on our journey as warrior moms.

Learning from the Matriarchs

In the Bible, we find many instances of matriarchs who experienced disappointments and setbacks. Consider Sarah, who endured years of barrenness before the birth of Isaac. Or Hannah, who grappled with infertility and the taunts of Peninnah before Samuel was born. Or Elizabeth, who was "advanced in years" before John the Baptist was conceived.

Each of these matriarchs faced significant disappointments and setbacks. Yet, in their stories, we see a demonstration of faith, resilience, and reliance on God. In their stories, we find encouragement for our journey, assurance for our struggles, and hope for our disappointments.

So, take heart from these matriarchs. Learn from their journey. Draw strength from their faith. And let their stories remind you that disappointments and setbacks are not the end. With God, they can become stepping stones to greater faith, deeper reliance, and profound grace.

Living in Victory

Despite the disappointments and setbacks, we live in victory. This doesn't mean we won't face disappointments or setbacks. Instead, it means that these experiences do not define us. They do not determine our standing with God, or our effectiveness as warrior moms.

Our victory is found in Christ. In His sacrificial love, His triumphant resurrection, His intercession for us. In Him, we are more than conquerors. In Him, we have the victory.

Therefore, in the face of disappointments and setbacks, let's cling to this victory. Let's rest in God's grace. Let's continue to stand, to fight, to intercede. Let's keep on being warrior moms - brave, resilient, grace-empowered mothers who advocate for their children, battle on their knees, and impact generations.

Disappointments and setbacks, while challenging, are part of our journey as warrior moms. But they do not define us. They do not deter us. With God's grace, they can mold us into more resilient warriors, more reliant mothers, more Christlike disciples.

In the face of disappointments and setbacks, let's remember this: We are human. We are held in God's love. We are helped by God's grace. And with His strength, we rise, we press on, we continue to fight.

So, warrior moms, let's keep going. Let's keep praying. Let's keep trusting. And let's keep living in victory, knowing that with God, no disappointment is wasted, no setback is insurmountable, and no battle is lost. In Him, we are victorious.

Chapter 31

Keeping the Faith: Trusting God in the Midst of Battle

As warrior moms, we find ourselves engaging in spiritual battles for the welfare of our children. In these intense moments, our faith can sometimes be stretched thin. The cacophony of the fight can deafen the whispers of our trust in God, and the blinding fog of warfare may overshadow the radiant light of His promises. However, the battlefield is where faith grows deepest roots, where trust in God is tested, solidified, and refined. In the midst of battle, our faith becomes the beacon of hope that shines, the shield that defends us, and the victory cry that propels us forward.

Understanding Faith in the Midst of Battle

Faith is not merely the assurance of what we hope for and the conviction of things unseen, as stated in Hebrews 11:1, but it is also a vibrant, living trust in God's character and His promises. It is this profound trust that we should maintain, especially in times of spiritual warfare. In the battleground, faith is not passive; it becomes dynamic, active, and alive. It's the spiritual lifeline that connects us with God, the trust that anchors us in His truth, and the conviction that propels us to move forward even in the face of uncertainties and adversities.

The Dynamics of Trusting God

Trust, an integral part of faith, can be described as the firm belief in the reliability, truth, or ability of someone or something. Trusting God, therefore, is having a firm belief in His reliability, His truth, and His ability. It is about believing that God is who He says He is, and that He will do what He says He will do.

Trusting God in the midst of spiritual battles involves two key dynamics: Surrender and Reliance.

1. Surrender: Surrender is the act of yielding ourselves completely to God. It's letting go of our need to control situations, releasing our fears and anxieties, and submitting ourselves fully to His sovereign will. In the midst of battle, surrender means acknowledging that we are not fighting in our strength, but in God's strength. It is recognizing our limitations and entrusting the outcome of the battle to God. When we surrender, we allow God to take the lead, to guide us, to fight for us, and to work on our behalf.

2. Reliance: Reliance is about depending on God and drawing strength from Him. It's about leaning on His promises, His power, His wisdom, and His love. In the battlefield, reliance means constantly seeking God's guidance, tapping into His strength, and declaring His promises over our situations. As we rely on God, we find the strength to endure, the wisdom to navigate, and the courage to confront our battles.

Both surrender and reliance work together in helping us trust God in the midst of spiritual battles. As we surrender to God, we become more reliant on Him. And as we rely on God, we find ourselves surrendering more to Him.

Nurturing Faith Amidst Battles

Nurturing faith in the midst of battles is about cultivating trust in God, and it involves three key elements:

1. Soaking in the Word: The Word of God is our spiritual nourishment. It's our guidebook for living and our manual for warfare. By constantly reading, meditating, and applying God's Word, we cultivate faith. His promises become our ammunition in battle, His commandments our strategy, and His truths our shield against the enemy's lies.

2. Persistent Prayer: Prayer is our direct line of communication with God. It's where we express our fears, pour out our hearts, and present our requests. But more than that, prayer is also where we listen to God, where we align ourselves with His will, and where we declare His promises over our situations. Persistent prayer not only helps us build a strong relationship with God, but it also strengthens our faith.

3. Fellowship with Believers: The community of faith is not just for companionship and comfort, but also for collective strength and corporate prayer. Fellowship with fellow believers can bolster our faith, offer

encouragement, provide wisdom, and invoke powerful intercession. In moments of battle, the shared faith, collective prayers, and combined spiritual strength of fellow believers can be instrumental.

Remembering God's Faithfulness

The Scripture is filled with stories of God's faithfulness. The Red Sea parting, the walls of Jericho falling, David defeating Goliath, Daniel surviving the lion's den, and countless other instances remind us that God is a promise-keeper. In our battles, it's important to remember God's past faithfulness, not just in biblical history, but also in our personal lives. Reflecting on how God has delivered us, provided for us, and guided us in the past can strengthen our faith and trust in Him amidst our current battles.

Walking in Faith

Walking in faith in the midst of battles is a spiritual journey. It involves steps of courage, strides of patience, climbs of endurance, and leaps of trust. But remember, we do not walk alone. God walks with us, guiding us, strengthening us, and fighting for us. With each step of faith, we are drawing closer to victory, for every battle fought in faith is already won in God's economy.

Faith is our spiritual vision in the battlefield. It allows us to see beyond the physical, to perceive the spiritual realities, and to envision the victory that

God has promised. And while the battleground may be fierce, our faith should be fiercer. For in the end, it is our faith, not our battles, that defines us.

In the spiritual battlefields for our children, as we wear the armor of God, wield the sword of the Spirit, and walk in faith, let's remember this: God is with us. He fights for us. He empowers us. And in Him, victory is assured. So, warrior moms, let's keep the faith. Let's trust God. Let's fight bravely. And let's march forward in victory. For in the end, it is not about the fierceness of the battle, but the faithfulness of our God.

Chapter 32

Victorious Legacy: Preparing to Pass on the Baton

Our journey as warrior moms, filled with fervent prayers, bold faith, and victorious battles, is not just for our benefit or our children's. Our mission extends beyond our immediate family; it reaches into the future generations, serving as a testament of God's faithfulness and a beacon for those coming after us. In this grand relay of life and faith, we are not just runners but also baton passers. This passage will delve into the importance of a victorious legacy and provide a roadmap for preparing to pass on the baton of faith and prayer.

The Baton of Faith and Prayer

The baton we hold is not just any baton. It is the baton of faith and prayer. This baton symbolizes the legacy of trusting in God, praying without ceasing, waging spiritual warfare, and experiencing divine victories. It represents the spiritual lessons we've learned, the faith we've cultivated, the prayers we've sown, and the victories we've garnered. It also encapsulates the hope we have in God, the courage we found in battles, and the love we've experienced from the Father.

The baton of faith and prayer, therefore, is not a trophy of past victories, but a tool for future battles. It's not a badge of honor, but a weapon of warfare. It's not an object of display, but a source of empowerment. As we prepare to pass on this baton, we need to ensure that it is well-equipped, battle-tested, and victory-guaranteed.

Preparing to Pass on the Baton

Preparing to pass on the baton involves more than merely waiting for the right time. It requires intentional preparation, conscious equipping, and purposeful impartation. This preparation process entails three key phases: Modeling, Mentoring, and Mobilizing.

1. Modeling: The first step in preparing to pass on the baton is modeling. It's about living out our faith and prayer in such a way that our children can see, learn, and follow. We need to exemplify a life of faith, a lifestyle of prayer, a spirit of resilience, and a heart for God. Our children should be able to witness how we trust God in times of trials, how we pray in moments of challenges, how we fight spiritual battles, and how we celebrate divine victories. This stage is not about teaching but living. It's not about telling but showing. It's not about instructing but embodying.

2. Mentoring: The second step is mentoring. Mentoring involves intentional teaching, guiding, and nurturing. This is where we explain the whys and hows of our faith and prayer. We teach our children how to trust God, how to pray effectively, how to discern spiritual realities, how to

wage spiritual warfare, and how to claim divine victories. We guide them in understanding biblical truths, in cultivating a relationship with God, and in navigating life's challenges. We nurture them to grow in faith, to mature in prayer, and to become victorious in their spiritual battles.

3. Mobilizing: The final step is mobilizing. This phase is about encouraging, empowering, and releasing our children to run their own race and fight their own battles. We encourage them to step out in faith, to pray for their own needs and battles, and to trust in God's faithfulness. We empower them with our testimonies of victories, with our experiences of God's faithfulness, and with our assurances of God's promises. And finally, we release them to run their race, to carry their baton, and to fight their battles. This stage is not about holding on but letting go. It's not about controlling but releasing. It's not about fearing but trusting.

The Journey Continues

As we pass on the baton, our role doesn't end; it transforms. We transition from being runners to being cheerleaders, from being warriors to being encouragers, from being teachers to being supporters. We continue to pray for them, to believe in them, and to stand with them. But now, we also celebrate their victories, learn from their experiences, and marvel at their faith.

In this journey of faith and prayer, the baton we pass on is not just a legacy of victories, but a heritage of faith, a lineage of prayer, and a dynasty of spiritual warriors. It's not just about what we've done, but about what God has done through us. It's not just about our battles, but about His victories. And as we pass on this baton, we are not just preparing our children for their races, but we are also propelling them towards their destinies.

So, warrior moms, as we prepare to pass on the baton, let's remember: Our race matters, our battles count, our victories inspire, and our legacy empowers. For the baton we pass on is not just a testament of our faith, but a catalyst for their victories. It's not just a reminder of our prayers, but a launchpad for their destinies. And in the grand relay of faith and prayer, every runner matters, every baton counts, every race inspires, and every victory empowers.

Chapter 33

Your Child, Your Heritage: Establishing the Spiritual Importance

A mother's heart beats in sync with her child's, from the first moment of awareness to the ongoing rhythm of life. This bond isn't merely biological; it carries a profound spiritual connection, transcending the limitations of the tangible world. When you became a mother, you were entrusted with more than a life to nurture and protect; you received a divine heritage, a precious soul destined for great purpose.

Your child, your heritage, is a God-given responsibility. Scripture paints a vivid picture in Psalm 127:3, declaring, "Behold, children are a heritage from the Lord, the fruit of the womb a reward." This is not a transient reward, something fleeting and temporal. No, it is an eternal gift, a divine endowment that resonates far beyond our earthly comprehension.

To grasp the significance of your child as your heritage, let's dive into the meaning of the term. The word 'heritage' in its biblical context suggests inheritance, legacy, and succession. This denotes a lineage that links the past, present, and future in a continuous chain. This, dear warrior mom, is the spiritual dimension you are called to uphold, defend, and nurture in your child.

Every child is a divine masterpiece, a unique blend of potential, purpose, and destiny, entrusted into the care of a chosen guardian—You, the warrior mom. The spiritual importance of this cannot be overstressed. Your child, created in the image of God (Genesis 1:27), carries a divine spark—an eternal soul destined for relationship with the Creator.

So, what is the role of a warrior mom in the spiritual journey of her child? It is to nourish, guard, and guide this divine spark towards its eternal destiny. This spiritual stewardship requires prayer, discernment, courage, and an unyielding faith. It demands you to rise as a warrior, fiercely protecting your child in the spiritual realm, a battleground often unseen but profoundly real.

Think of Hannah, the mother of Samuel in the Bible (1 Samuel 1). Amidst the anguish of barrenness, she poured her heart out to God, promising to dedicate her child to His service if He granted her a son. Her fervent prayers bore fruit, and Samuel was born. Hannah kept her promise, nurturing Samuel's spiritual growth, which led him to become one of Israel's greatest prophets. Her role as a warrior mom was vital, not only to Samuel but to the entire nation of Israel.

Or, consider Mary, the mother of Jesus Christ. Her faith, courage, and unwavering commitment to the divine plan, even when it brought her immeasurable pain, epitomize the spirit of a warrior mom. Mary's willingness to participate in God's divine plan, to nurture and protect Jesus, played a pivotal role in the salvation narrative.

Your children, like Samuel and Jesus, carry divine assignments. As their mother, your role extends beyond the physical realm of providing care and affection. You are to recognize, foster, and defend the divine spark within them. This implies immersing yourself in ceaseless prayer, teaching them the Word of God, modeling a life of faith, and intervening in the spiritual realm when battles arise.

In Deuteronomy 6:6-9, the Bible offers explicit instructions to parents: "These commandments that I give you today are to be on your hearts. Impress them on your children. Talk about them when you sit at home and when you walk along the road, when you lie down and when you get up." Here, the mandate for spiritual parenting is clear. You are to imprint God's truths onto your child's heart, making it an integral part of their life's rhythm.

Imagine your child as an empty vessel, a masterpiece in the making. Your words, actions, prayers, and the spiritual environment you create, fill this vessel. The value of the divine truths you instill, the faith-filled atmospheres you cultivate, and the spiritual battles you fight on their behalf, shape the course of their destiny. This is the weighty, yet glorious calling of a warrior mom.

The spiritual development of a child is akin to the growth of a seed. Planted in the fertile soil of prayer, watered with the Word of God, protected from the harsh elements of sin and darkness, the divine seed in your child can sprout, grow, and bear fruits of righteousness. As a warrior mom, you are both the diligent farmer and the protective hedge around this young sapling.

Remember, dear warrior mom, spiritual battles are won on bended knees, and victory is claimed in the name of Jesus. Ephesians 6:12 reminds us, "For our struggle is not against flesh and blood, but against the rulers, against the authorities, against the powers of this dark world and against the spiritual forces of evil in the heavenly realms." Recognizing this spiritual warfare and standing firm in the authority of Christ is pivotal to defend your child in the court of heaven.

In conclusion, the spiritual significance of your role as a mother is immense. You are not merely shaping an individual; you are influencing an eternal soul, crafting a divine destiny, and impacting generations to come. Your child is your heritage, an eternal gift from God. Recognize this truth, embrace your role as a warrior mom, and remember, your most potent weapon in this spiritual journey is unwavering faith in God. May you rise in His strength, fight with His wisdom, and triumph in His name, for the spiritual destiny of your child.

Chapter 34

In the Trenches:
Recognizing the Signs of Spiritual Warfare

As a warrior mom, you are entrusted with the task of discerning not only the physical but also the spiritual climate surrounding your children. It is a battlefield out there, one that operates in dimensions unseen by the human eye but felt profoundly by the spirit. This is where you fight - in the trenches of spiritual warfare.

In the vast realm of spiritual warfare, your senses must remain alert, your mind discerning, and your spirit fortified. Recognition of the battle signs is a crucial first step in defending your children effectively. To recognize, however, you must first understand. So, let's plunge deep into the trenches of this unseen war.

In Ephesians 6:12, the Apostle Paul vividly outlines the dimensions of our struggle: "For our struggle is not against flesh and blood, but against the rulers, against the authorities, against the powers of this dark world and against the spiritual forces of evil in the heavenly realms." These forces - rulers, authorities, powers of darkness, and spiritual forces of evil - embody the entities of spiritual warfare. Recognizing their influence in your children's lives calls for spiritual discernment, a skill that is honed through persistent prayer and intimate knowledge of God's Word.

Let's explore the signs of spiritual warfare, those subtle indicators that signal a spiritual battle brewing in your child's life. Although not exhaustive, these signs offer a practical guide to spotting the enemy's tactics, preparing you to engage in effective spiritual combat.

1. Unusual Fear or Anxiety: Fear and anxiety are potent weapons in the enemy's arsenal. If your child is exhibiting unusual fear or anxiety, it might indicate a spiritual attack. While it's normal for children to have fears, be on the lookout for inexplicable, persistent dread or panic that seems out of character or context.

2. Sudden Changes in Behavior or Personality: An abrupt alteration in your child's behavior, such as aggression, withdrawal, or an unusual lack of joy, could indicate a spiritual battle. This doesn't discount the possibility of natural causes like hormonal changes or stress. However, if these changes persist without apparent cause, it might signify spiritual warfare.

3. Rebellion Against Authority: Rebellion often signals a struggle for control, a hallmark of spiritual warfare. If your child shows sudden, strong rebellion against authority—be it parental, school, or other legitimate authorities—this could indicate spiritual turmoil.

4. Extreme Fatigue: Unusual, extreme fatigue, or lack of energy that isn't related to physical causes can sometimes be a sign of spiritual warfare. The enemy often uses weariness to make us less vigilant, to lower our defenses.

5. Obsession with Darkness: If your child shows an increasing fascination with dark themes—through music, movies, books, or friendships—it might indicate a spiritual battle. This isn't to say that every interest in these themes equates to spiritual warfare, but a noticeable, intense obsession can be a warning sign.

6. Lack of Interest in Spiritual Things: A sudden disinterest in prayer, Bible reading, church, or spiritual conversations might suggest a spiritual struggle. Apathy towards God and spiritual matters is a tactic of the enemy to create distance between us and our Creator.

Recognizing these signs is only the beginning. You, warrior mom, are not just a passive observer but an active participant in this spiritual warfare. Armed with the recognition of the enemy's tactics, you can proceed to counteract his strategies, defend your child, and reclaim any lost ground. Your response to these signs is pivotal. Ephesians 6:13-14 advises, "Therefore put on the full armor of God, so that when the day of evil comes, you may be able to stand your ground, and after you have done everything, to stand. Stand firm then..."

Engaging in this warfare, you have an arsenal at your disposal: the Word of God, prayer, faith, and the power of the Holy Spirit. When signs of spiritual warfare become evident, combat fear with the truth of God's Word, affirming that "God has not given us a spirit of fear, but of power and of love and of a sound mind" (2 Timothy 1:7).

Combat sudden behavioral changes with prayer, interceding for your child's mind to be renewed and their heart softened. Address rebellion against authority by praying for a spirit of humility and obedience, reminding them of the wisdom in respecting authority as it says in Romans 13:1, "Let everyone be subject to the governing authorities, for there is no authority except that which God has established."

Counteract extreme fatigue by encouraging rest and providing a peaceful environment, fortified with prayers for renewed strength and energy. The Psalmist affirms in Psalm 46:10, "Be still, and know that I am God;" in the stillness, God revives us.

Confront an obsession with darkness by exposing your child to the light of God's love and truth. Continuously share about God's love, His goodness, and His plans for their life. "The light shines in the darkness, and the darkness has not overcome it" (John 1:5).

Finally, tackle a lack of interest in spiritual things by creating a vibrant spiritual atmosphere at home. Make prayer, Bible study, and worship a regular part of your family routine. The family that prays together stays together, united under God's protection.

In the trenches of spiritual warfare, recognizing the signs of the enemy's attack equips you, the warrior mom, for the battle at hand. However, remember, the battleground is not your home; it's merely the terrain on which you fight. Your home is in the victory, the triumph secured by Christ at the cross. As you navigate this terrain, always hold on to the promise that "The one who is in you is greater than the one who is in the world" (1 John 4:4). You fight from victory, not for victory. Stand firm, warrior mom. The battle belongs to the Lord.

Chapter 35

Intercession: Praying with Purpose and Power

On the battleground of spiritual warfare, prayer is your weapon of choice. More than mere words whispered into the wind, prayer is a dynamic dialogue with the Creator of the Universe. It is your spiritual lifeline, connecting you with the Source of all power. But as a warrior mom, you're called to a specific type of prayer: intercession.

Intercession, in its simplest form, is praying on behalf of others. It is standing in the gap, pleading before God for someone else's needs. When it comes to your children, intercession takes on an even deeper level of urgency and purpose. You're not just praying; you're waging spiritual war, defending your children in the court of heaven.

The Bible is rich with examples of intercessory prayer. Moses interceded for the Israelites. Esther interceded for her people. Paul interceded for the churches under his care. Jesus Himself interceded - and continues to intercede - for us. Following their example, you're to intercede for your children, becoming their advocate before God.

Yet, to intercede with power and purpose, there are certain principles you must understand. Let's delve into the dynamics of intercession, guiding you to pray effectively for your children.

1. Pray with Authority: As a believer in Christ, you've been given spiritual authority. In Luke 10:19, Jesus says, "I have given you authority to trample on snakes and scorpions and to overcome all the power of the enemy; nothing will harm you." Exercise this authority in prayer, confidently standing against any forces that threaten your children's spiritual well-being.

2. Pray with Specificity: When interceding for your children, be specific in your prayers. Pray for their spiritual growth, for their protection, for their friendships, for their future. Name their struggles before God. The more specific you are, the more targeted your prayers become.

3. Pray with Persistence: Intercession isn't a one-time event; it's an ongoing commitment. In Luke 18:1, Jesus told his disciples a parable to show them that they should always pray and not give up. Keep praying for your children, even when you don't immediately see results.

4. Pray with Expectation: Pray with the expectation that God will move. Believe that He hears and answers prayers. Remember, you serve a God for whom nothing is impossible. Hebrews 11:1 affirms, "Now faith is confidence in what we hope for and assurance about what we do not see."

5. Pray with Scripture: Use the Bible as your prayer guide. Pray God's promises over your children. His Word is alive and powerful (Hebrews 4:12), and when you pray in line with His Word, you align yourself with His will.

With these principles in mind, let's consider some practical ways to pray for your children.

1. Pray for Their Salvation: The most important prayer you can pray for your children is for their salvation. Intercede that they will come to a saving knowledge of Jesus Christ. Pray that they would understand their need for a Savior and respond to God's offer of forgiveness and eternal life.

2. Pray for Their Spiritual Growth: Intercede for your children's spiritual growth. Pray that they would grow in their knowledge and understanding of God's Word. Ask God to help them develop a deep love for Him and a desire to live in a way that pleases Him.

3. Pray for Their Protection: As a warrior mom, one of your primary roles is to pray for your children's protection. Pray for their physical safety, but also for their spiritual protection. Pray that they would be shielded from the influences of the world and the attacks of the enemy.

4. Pray for Their Relationships: Pray for your children's relationships, both with peers and adults. Pray for godly friends who will encourage them in

their faith. Pray for wise mentors who can guide them. Pray for their future spouse, if they are to have one.

5. Pray for Their Purpose: Each of your children is unique, created by God for a specific purpose. Intercede for them to discover and embrace God's plan for their lives. Pray that they would use their gifts and talents for God's glory.

Intercession is a powerful tool in spiritual warfare. As a warrior mom, your prayers can make a significant impact in the spiritual realm. Never underestimate the power of a praying mother. Stand in the gap for your children. Fight for them in the spiritual realm. Your prayers are heard. Your prayers matter. So, keep praying, warrior mom. Your prayers are shaping the spiritual destiny of your children.

Chapter 36

Building Spiritual Walls: Defending Your Family from Attacks

Spiritual warfare is a reality, and the threats it poses are not merely individual, they often target families. In this invisible battle, your family home is not just a physical structure; it's a spiritual fortress. Within its walls, faith is nurtured, prayers are lifted, and God's Word is honored. As a warrior mom, you have a crucial role in building and maintaining the spiritual walls of this fortress, providing a defensive barrier against the enemy's attacks.

The concept of building spiritual walls is not a novel idea. In the Old Testament, the city of Jerusalem had physical walls for protection. When these walls were broken down, the inhabitants were vulnerable to enemy attacks. Nehemiah, a cupbearer to the king, was divinely assigned the task of rebuilding these walls. This physical rebuilding carries powerful spiritual parallels for your task of building spiritual walls around your family.

The process of building spiritual walls involves several key elements:

1. Laying the Foundation: The foundation of your spiritual walls is Jesus Christ. He is the cornerstone, the starting point for all spiritual defense. Establishing your family's faith in Jesus and His finished work on the cross is the first step in building your spiritual walls. As it is written, "For no one can lay any foundation other than the one already laid, which is Jesus Christ" (1 Corinthians 3:11).

2. Building with Prayer: Prayer is the bricks and mortar of your spiritual walls. It is through prayer that you engage with God and invoke His protective presence over your family. Regular, heartfelt prayer sessions, both individually and as a family, fortify your walls. As Paul instructed in Ephesians 6:18, "And pray in the Spirit on all occasions with all kinds of prayers and requests."

3. Implementing the Word: The Word of God serves as the reinforcing steel within your spiritual walls, giving them strength and stability. Immerse your family in the Scriptures. Teach them, discuss them, and encourage your children to hide God's Word in their hearts. "I have hidden your word in my heart that I might not sin against you" (Psalm 119:11).

4. Encouraging Righteous Living: Righteous living is the protective coating on your spiritual walls. As your family chooses to live in obedience to God's Word, you close doors to the enemy's attacks. "For the eyes of the Lord are on the righteous and his ears are attentive to their prayer, but the face of the Lord is against those who do evil" (1 Peter 3:12).

5. Cultivating Love and Unity: Love and unity among family members add an additional layer of protection to your spiritual walls. Where there is unity, God commands a blessing (Psalm 133:3). Strive to cultivate a family environment where love, forgiveness, and unity thrive.

Maintaining the spiritual walls around your family requires constant vigilance. Like a watchman on the city walls, be alert to potential breaches. Recognize areas of vulnerability and address them promptly. These may include persistent sin, negative influences, harmful media content, or divisive relationships.

Remember, the goal of building spiritual walls isn't to isolate your family from the world, but to insulate them from the enemy's attacks. Your task is not to create a spiritual bubble that prevents your children from engaging with the world, but to build a spiritual fortress that equips them to engage with the world from a position of strength and victory.

In this endeavor, you're not alone. The Holy Spirit is your helper and guide. Moreover, the Master Builder Himself, God, is committed to the safety and wellbeing of your family. As He promised in Isaiah 49:25,

"I will contend with those who contend with you, and your children I will save."

So, warrior mom, rise up and build. Your family's spiritual defense depends on it.

Chapter 37

The Art of Spiritual Self-Care: Nourishing the Warrior Within

Even the mightiest warrior needs rest and rejuvenation. While the call of a warrior mom is noble and powerful, it requires immense spiritual energy and stamina. If not properly cared for, even the strongest soldier can grow weary. Spiritual self-care, therefore, is not a luxury; it's a necessity. Nourishing the warrior within is about more than just occasional moments of relaxation; it's about a sustainable lifestyle that regularly replenishes your spiritual reserves.

Spiritual self-care is the intentional practice of nurturing your spiritual well-being. It encompasses all the activities and habits that feed your soul, uplift your spirit, deepen your relationship with God, and enhance your resilience in spiritual warfare. It is about prioritizing your spiritual health, understanding that a nourished spirit makes a powerful warrior.

The concept of self-care is often misunderstood, sometimes dismissed as selfish indulgence or unnecessary luxury. However, scriptural principles affirm the importance of spiritual self-care. Jesus Himself often withdrew to solitary places to pray (Luke 5:16). He understood the importance of nourishing His spirit, staying connected to the Father, and maintaining His spiritual vitality.

So, what does spiritual self-care look like for a warrior mom? How do you nourish the warrior within? Here are some key practices:

1. Prioritize Time with God: Amid the demands of motherhood, setting aside time for God can seem challenging. Yet, spending time with God is the most important aspect of spiritual self-care. Make it a priority. Create a regular time and place for prayer, Bible reading, and quiet reflection. This time of communion with God renews your spirit, brings perspective, and fuels your spiritual strength.

2. Engage in Worship: Worship is a powerful form of spiritual self-care. It takes the focus off your battles and places it on God. Regularly engage in worship, whether through music, prayer, or other creative expressions. Worship cultivates a heart of gratitude and fosters a deeper connection with God.

3. Practice Mindfulness: Mindfulness, the practice of being fully present in the moment, has profound spiritual benefits. It helps quiet the noise of life, enabling you to hear God's voice more clearly. Practice mindfulness in your devotions, your chores, and even your interactions with your children. "Be still, and know that I am God" (Psalm 46:10).

4. Connect with a Faith Community: Your spiritual health thrives in community. Regular interaction with a faith community provides spiritual support, encouragement, and accountability. Attend a local church, join a Bible study group, or connect with other Christian moms. These relationships can be a source of spiritual nourishment.

5. Nurture Your Spiritual Gifts: Each believer has been given spiritual gifts (1 Corinthians 12). Nurturing these gifts is a form of spiritual self-care. Whether your gifts lie in teaching, serving, encouraging, or any other area, find ways to utilize and develop them. Doing so not only benefits others but also brings joy and fulfillment to your own spirit.

6. Pursue Spiritual Growth: Spiritual self-care involves ongoing spiritual growth. Commit to becoming a lifelong learner of God's Word. Attend Bible studies, read Christian literature, listen to sermons and Christian podcasts. Continually growing in your understanding of God and His Word strengthens your spirit and equips you for spiritual warfare.

7. Take Care of Your Physical Health: The apostle Paul reminded us that our bodies are temples of the Holy Spirit (1 Corinthians 6:19). Taking care of your physical health is, therefore, a form of spiritual self-care. Regular exercise, proper nutrition, and adequate sleep can enhance your spiritual well-being by increasing your energy, improving your mood, and reducing stress.

8. Embrace Rest: God designed the principle of Sabbath for our benefit. Regularly taking time to rest is a crucial aspect of spiritual self-care. Rest is not just about physical relaxation; it's about spiritual rejuvenation. Use your times of rest to disconnect from the demands of life and reconnect with God.

Remember, warrior mom, you can't pour from an empty cup. Taking care of your spiritual well-being is not selfish; it's necessary. By nourishing the warrior within, you not only enhance your own spiritual health but also become a stronger spiritual guardian for your children.

May you, like the apostle Paul, run the race with perseverance, not growing weary but constantly renewed by the Spirit of God. "But those who hope in the LORD will renew their strength. They will soar on wings like eagles; they will run and not grow weary, they will walk and not be faint" (Isaiah 40:31). So, embrace the art of spiritual self-care, and keep your inner warrior strong and ready for battle.

Chapter 38

Navigating Seasons of Warfare: Understanding the Spiritual Calendar

Spiritual warfare is not a constant, static battle. It ebbs and flows like the changing seasons, with varying intensities and focus. As a warrior mom, it's essential to understand the spiritual calendar, to discern the specific seasons of warfare, and to navigate them with wisdom and discernment. By recognizing the spiritual climate and adjusting your strategies accordingly, you can effectively defend your family in every season.

The concept of a spiritual calendar may seem unconventional, but it is grounded in biblical principles. Ecclesiastes 3:1 tells us, "There is a time for everything, and a season for every activity under the heavens." This principle applies to spiritual warfare as well. Just as the physical world experiences different seasons, so does the spiritual realm.

To navigate the seasons of warfare, it's important to identify and understand the characteristics of each season. While these seasons may not follow a fixed timetable, they can be discerned through spiritual sensitivity and discernment. Here are some key seasons of warfare to be aware of:

1. Preparation Season: This is a season of preparation, where God equips and strengthens you for what lies ahead. It's a time of drawing closer to Him, deepening your prayer life, and saturating yourself in His Word. In this season, God reveals strategies and imparts wisdom to navigate the battles to come. Embrace this season of preparation, for it lays a solid foundation for the battles ahead.

2. Intensified Warfare Season: This season is marked by increased spiritual opposition and battles on multiple fronts. It's a time when the enemy seeks to hinder your progress and undermine your faith. During intensified warfare, you may encounter challenges in various areas of your life, including relationships, health, and finances. This is a critical season that requires unwavering faith and reliance on God's strength.

3. Season of Breakthrough: After enduring intense warfare, God often ushers in a season of breakthrough. This is a time of victories, answered prayers, and divine favor. It's a season where the enemy's strongholds are shattered, and God's purposes are advanced. In this season, continue to press forward in faith, for breakthrough is on the horizon.

4. Rest and Restoration Season: Just as physical seasons include times of rest and rejuvenation, so does the spiritual calendar. This season is marked by rest, refreshing, and restoration. It's a time to recharge, heal from battle wounds, and reconnect with God. Embrace this season and allow God to replenish your spirit, filling you with new strength for the seasons ahead.

5. Season of Promotion and Advancement: This is a season of elevation and advancement in the spiritual realm. God may open doors of opportunity, release new assignments, or bring forth a greater manifestation of your spiritual gifts. Stay attuned to God's leading and walk in obedience, for He is positioning you for greater impact in the spiritual battles to come.

6. Harvest Season: In the natural world, harvest season is a time of reaping the fruits of labor. In the spiritual realm, it represents a season of reaping spiritual harvest. It's a time when prayers are answered, souls are saved, and God's purposes come to fruition. Be expectant in this season and continue to sow seeds of prayer, love, and truth, for a bountiful harvest awaits.

Navigating these seasons requires spiritual sensitivity and discernment. Here are some practical steps to help you navigate the seasons of warfare effectively:

1. Seek God's Wisdom: Cultivate a deep relationship with God through prayer, meditation on His Word, and listening to the leading of the Holy Spirit. Seek His wisdom and guidance in discerning the seasons and understanding the strategies to employ.

2. Stay Rooted in God's Word: The Bible is your compass in navigating the spiritual seasons. Meditate on God's promises, declarations, and instructions. Let His Word guide your actions, decisions, and prayers.

3. Maintain Consistent Spiritual Practices: Regardless of the season, maintain consistent spiritual practices such as prayer, worship, and fellowship with other believers. These practices keep you connected to God's presence and strengthen your spiritual foundation.

4. Remain Flexible and Adaptable: The spiritual seasons may not align with your expectations or plans. Stay flexible and adaptable, allowing God to direct your steps and adjust your strategies as needed.

5. Surround Yourself with a Supportive Community: Join with other believers who understand the reality of spiritual warfare. Share your experiences, seek counsel, and pray together. A supportive community provides encouragement and accountability in navigating the seasons.

6. Embrace Spiritual Disciplines: Engage in fasting, spiritual retreats, and other disciplines that draw you closer to God and strengthen your spiritual resolve. These practices heighten your sensitivity to the spiritual seasons and deepen your connection with God.

Remember, warrior mom, the spiritual battles you face are not random or aimless. They occur within the context of the spiritual calendar. By understanding and navigating these seasons with wisdom and discernment, you can effectively defend your family and advance God's kingdom. Trust in the Lord's guidance, remain steadfast in prayer, and be confident that He who began a good work in you will carry it on to completion.

Appreciation

Thank you for purchasing and reading my book. I am extremely grateful and hope you found value in reading it. Please consider sharing it with friends and family and leaving a review online.

Your feedback and support are always appreciated and allow me to continue doing what I love.

Please go to https://www.amazon.com/dp/B0CFX87CB2 if you'd like to leave a review.

TIMOTHY ATUNNISE's BESTSELLERS

Deliverance & Spiritual Warfare
- Monitoring spirits exposed and defeated
- Jezebel spirit exposed and defeated
- Marine spirits exposed and defeated
- Prophetic warfare: Unleashing supernatural power in warfare
- Rise above the curse: An empowering guide to overcome witchcraft attacks
- The time is now: A guide to overcoming marital delay
- Earth moving prayers: Pray until miracles happen
- I must win this battle: Expanded edition
- I must my financial battle
- Essential prayers
- Open heavens: Unlocking divine blessings and breakthroughs
- This battle ends now
- Breaking the unbreakable
- Reversing evil handwriting
- I must win this battle - French edition
- I must win this battle - Spanish edition
- Ammunition for spiritual warfare
- Reversing the Irreversible
- Let there be a change
- Total Deliverance: Volume 1
- 21 days prayer for total breakthroughs
- Warrior Mom: Defending your children in the court of heaven

Weapons of Warfare
- The Name of Jesus: The unstoppable weapon of warfare
- Praise and Worship: Potent weapons of warfare
- Blood of Jesus: The ultimate weapon

- The Word of God as a weapon: A double-edged sword to bring transformation and unparallel victory in spiritual warfare.
- Praying with Power: The warrior's guide to weapon of dynamic warfare prayer
- The weapon of prophetic dreams

14 Days Prayer & Fasting Series
- 14 Days prayer to break evil patterns.
- 14 days prayer against delay and stagnation
- 14 days prayer for a new beginning
- 14 days prayer for deliverance from demonic attacks
- 14 days prayer for total healing
- 14 days prayer for deliverance from rejection and hatred
- 14 days prayer for healing the foundations
- 14 days prayer for breaking curses and evil covenants
- 14 days prayer for uncommon miracles
- 14 days prayer for restoration and total recovery
- 14 days prayer: It's time for a change
- 14 days prayer for deliverance from witchcraft attacks
- 14 days prayer for accelerated promotion
- 14 days prayer for deliverance from generational problems
- 14 days prayer for supernatural supply
- 14 days prayer to God's will for your life
- 14 days prayer for Mountaintop Experience
- 14 days prayer for home, family and marriage restoration
- 14 days prayer to overcome stubborn situations
- 14 days prayer for financial breakthroughs

Personal Finances
- The art of utility bills negotiation
- From strapped to successful: Unlocking financial freedom beyond Paycheck to paycheck
- Escape the rat race: How to retire in five years or less

Bible Study
- The King is coming
- Seven judgments of the Bible
- The miracle of Jesus Christ
- The book of Exodus
- Lost and found: The house of Israel
- The parables of Jesus Christ

Fiction
- The merchant's legacy: A tale of faith and family
- A world unraptured: Brink of oblivion
- Gone: A chronicle of chaos

Family Counseling
- Healing whispers: Biblical comfort and healing for men after miscarriage

Leadership/Business
- The most intelligent woman: A woman's guide to outsmarting any room at any level
- Thriving in the unknown: Preparing children for careers that don't exist yet
- Communication breakthrough: Cultivating deep connections through active listening
- Overcoming Procrastination

Theology/Ministry
- Laughing Pulpit: Using humor to enhance preaching.

Parenting/Relationship

- Embracing metamorphosis: Nurturing teenage girls' remarkable journey into adulthood

Marriage/Family
- The conscious husband: Mastering active listening in marriage.
- The conscious wife: Nurturing relationship with awareness, building a perfect and flourishing family.
- Conscious parenting: Mastering active listening to your children.
- From cradle to consciousness: Guiding your child's awareness
- The 'Not Tonight' syndrome: Overcoming false excuses in marital intimacy.

End-Times
- Dawn of eternity: Unraveling the rapture of the saints
- Signs of the end-times: Deciphering prophecies in a race against time
- The rise of the Antichrist: Unveiling the beast and the prophecies

Made in United States
Orlando, FL
04 January 2024